Best
Tea Shop Walks
in Nottinghamshire

Paul & Sandra Biggs

Do bear in mind that establishments are subject to change. We strongly recommend that you telephone beforehand to ensure that the tea shop is open. It would be a disaster should the establishment be closed on your intended visit, due to an unexpected emergency. Tea shops are usually maintained to the highest of standards. Some have luxuriously fitted carpets, others are immaculately clean. Please respect cleanliness and remove muddy boots before entering. It may be an idea to carry a pair of shoes or trainers in a rucksack with you, if the tea shop is not at the end of the walk, and you intend calling at some point along the route.

The Country Code

* Enjoy the countryside and respect its life and work.
* Guard against all risks of fire.
* Leave gates as you find them.
* Keep your dogs under close control.
* Keep to public footpaths across farmland.
* Use gates and stiles to cross fences, hedges and walls.
* Leave livestock, crops and machinery alone.
* Take your litter home.
* Help to keep all water clean.
* Protect wildlife, plants and trees.
* Take special care on country roads.
* Make no unnecessary noise.

Tourist Information Centres

Mansfield – Old Town Hall, Market Place, Mansfield, Nottinghamshire, NG18 1HX. Tel: 01623 427770.

Newark – Gilstrap Centre, Castlegate, Newark, Nottinghamshire, NG24 1BG. Tel: 01636 678962.

Nottingham – 1-4 Smithy Row, Nottingham, NG1 2BY. Tel: 0115 915 5330.

Ollerton – Sherwood Heath, Ollerton Roundabout, Ollerton, Newark, Nottinghamshire, NG22 9DR. Tel: 01623 824545.

Retford – Arncott House, Grove Street, Retford, Nottinghamshire, DN22 6JU. Tel: 01777 860780.

Sherwood Forest – Sherwood Forest Visitor Centre, Edwinstowe near Mansfield, Nottinghamshire, NG21 9HN. Tel: 01623 824490/823202.

West Bridgford – County Hall, Loughborough Road, West Bridgford, Nottingham, NG2 7QP. Tel: 0115 977 3558.

Worksop – Public Library, Memorial Avenue, Worksop, Nottinghamshire, S80 2BP. Tel: 01909 501148.

Public Transport

There was a time when public transport was only used by those without a car, but today things are changing. People are now rediscovering trains and buses, and finding they can be a better way to get about. Everyone can help to make a difference, not by abandoning our cars, but by using them less when it is possible to do so - why not go 'green' for a day. All of the walks can be reached by public transport, with full details given in the fact file for each walk. On the rare occasion where there is no service to coincide with the starting point, we have given an alternative suggestion where to start the walk, in order that public transport may be taken.

For information on all bus services in Nottinghamshire, including summer leisure services to major attractions, call the Buses "Hotline" on 0115 924 0000. Nottinghamshire County Council sponsors this telephone service and, provided timetables are available for the service you require, one will be forwarded free of charge.

A good rail network exists in the county with mainline stations at Nottingham, Newark and Alfreton/Mansfield Parkway. Since the privatisation of railways, a number of changes have occurred to the network. Midland Mainline operate the London St Pancras – Nottingham service, while Virgin is in charge of the Kings Cross – Edinburgh service that calls at Newark. Central Trains Ltd control all cross country trains including the Robin Hood line that links Nottingham with Mansfield and Worksop. For details of services in Nottingham, telephone the National Rail Enquiries at Derby on 0345484950. They are sponsored by all of the different rail companies to give impartial advice on national and local rail services.

Walk 1. Worksop

Route: Tourist Information Centre – Worksop – St Anne church – Worksop Manor – South Lodge – Manor Hills – Drinking Pit Lane – Truman's Lodge – Clumber Old Wood – College Pines Golf Course – Worksop College – Manton – Gatehouse – Priory Church – Worksop – Tourist Information Centre.

Start: The Tourist Information Centre, Worksop Library and Museum, Memorial Avenue, Worksop. Grid reference 589789.

Distance: 8½ miles.

Maps: OS Landranger 120, Mansfield, Worksop and surrounding area; OS Explorer 28, Sherwood Forest.

Terrain: Excellent going underfoot along field paths and broad woodland tracks. Steady climb over the Manor Hills. Some road walking around Worksop.

Public Transport: Worksop can be reached by bus from Mansfield, Doncaster, Retford, Nottingham and Chesterfield. Services are fairly frequent, Monday – Saturday, but a curtailed service on Sundays. Mainly operated by Stagecoach but other companies such as Unity Coaches and Lincs Road Car also run services. There is a railway station at Worksop. The Robin Hood line runs between Nottingham and Worksop. Also services from Sheffield to Lincoln call.

By Car: The best approach to Worksop is along the A57 from either the A1 or A60. Main roads from all neighbouring towns and villages make it very easy to get to the town. Plenty of long and short stay car parks in Worksop. The ideal car park is on Memorial Avenue, adjacent to the public library.

The Tea Shop

The Coffee Bean on Watson Road in Worksop is tucked away just off the main shopping thoroughfare, a short distance from the Tourist Information Centre. The proprietor and chef is Paul Knight, who has owned the business since April 1997. He works extremely hard, as he is responsible for all the succulent dishes that are available on the menu.

Inside, the coffee shop is decorated on the lines of a Tudor building with black painted oak beams. The previous owners called the coffee shop 'The Tudor' but when Paul took over he thought The Coffee Bean was more appropriate. There is seating for 36, at nine tables, in the quaint surroundings. The coffee shop is enhanced with prints, old jugs, plates and tins on the walls.

Looking at the menu, at the tempting fare, you are spoilt for choice. Above the serving counter is a blackboard with 'specials'. A full English Breakfast is served until 11am, although an all day breakfast is available. If peckish between 9.00am and 11.00am, try the morning spread which offers a choice of toast, crumpets, muffins or croissant with tea or coffee. An excellent choice of lunches such as gammon, pork chop, mixed grill, sirloin steak or scampi all served with chips, peas and a salad garni, will keep you nicely 'topped up' for the day. If you fancy a lighter lunch, why not go for the omelette, jacket potato, baguette, toasties, sandwiches or burgers, which are home-made, served in a bun with salad. Paul makes all the cakes and pastries, and the Afternoon Special is a real bargain. A slice of home-made cake and tea or coffee with a free top up is very reasonable. In fact, all the prices are extremely satisfactory, and there is no doubt that the Coffee Bean offers exceptional value for money.

Opening Hours: 9.00am to 4.00pm, Monday to Saturday; Closed Sundays. Phone: 01909 477761.

Worksop

The name Worksop is an ancient one with over 60 different spellings of the word, including the Saxon term of 'Worchesope'. Other variations recorded are 'Worsoppe' and 'Worstop'. There are plenty of different meanings to the names but the most likely is thought to be " a fortified hill" or earthworks, such as Castle Hill. From the Domesday survey, it was seen that Worksop was a prosperous settlement, owing to its location being close to the Royal Forest of Sherwood. Many Kings, Queens and distinguished figures often visited Worksop during this period of history.

Worksop's past is linked to coal mining. The town is also famous for Windsor chair making, liquorice growing, and brewing. On August 26 1931, Worksop was granted its Charter by King George V. The borough's coat of arms features many elements of significance to the town including a knight in armour, a forester with a longbow, an oak tree, a lion, five ducal coronets and a miner's pick and shovel.

Worksop, today, is known as the northern gateway to the Dukeries. The town centre is attractively pedestrianised on a ducal theme. In 1990 this original scheme, designed by the County Council's Landscape group, won a prestigious national award for Worksop. The Town Hall dates from 1851 and was built as the Corn Exchange. Behind it were slaughterhouses for the nearby market. The market place was originally surrounded by buildings, including shops and inns, and was entered through two narrow lanes. The market cross, from which all milestones were measured, stood here at the top of Bridge Street.

Worksop Museum

Housed in the library on Memorial Avenue, along with the tourist information office, this listed building is a fine example of 1930s architecture. At the outbreak of the Second World War, it was used as the Worksop and District Food Office. The museum currently only contains the 'Pilgrim Fathers' story, as

Walk 2. Retford

Route: Retford Bus Station – Chesterfield Canal – Whitsunday Pie Lock – East Retford – Brick and Tile Inn – Sinclairs Coffee Shop – Retford Bus Station.

Start: The Bus Station, Beardsalls Row, Retford. Grid reference 708809.

Distance: 4 Miles.

Maps: OS Landranger 120, Mansfield, Worksop and surrounding area; OS Pathfinder 745, East Retford (North) and Blyth.

Terrain: Grassy towpath, Chesterfield Canal. Good clear footpaths across fields. Town Centre Trail. No steep climbs.

Public Transport: Retford is well served by buses from Doncaster, Mansfield and Worksop operated by Lincs Road Car and Stagecoach. There are two railway stations served by train services from London Kings Cross/Edinburgh and Sheffield/Gainsborough/Lincoln.

By Car: The best route is to use the A1 then take the A620 into Retford from the north and west. Alternatively use the A638 from Markham Moor if approaching from the south and east. There are a number of pay and display car parks in Retford although some are short stay only.

The Tea Shop

Sinclairs Coffee Shop is situated on the first floor of Sinclairs China Shop in The Square, close to the market. The elegant three-storey building dates from Victorian times having been used as a Doctor's house. Previously it was a DSS office. When John Sinclair bought the building it was derelict and he lavishly restored each floor into today's palatial surroundings. In 1985 the coffee shop opened along with the china, crystal and luxuries shop. The 'in store' coffee shop has an extremely high standard of cuisine and comfort, complimented by waitress service. Marian Holland is the manageress of the coffee shop, and she ensures the smooth running of the establishment is maintained.

A really excellent selection of home-made dishes and cakes are available everyday. Lunches are served between 12.00 noon – 2.30pm, consisting of such filling fayre as Stilton and apple ploughman's, duck and orange paté, quiche, salads, home-made soup with bacon, lettuce and tomato cob and a dish of the day which is written on a board. Jacket Potatoes, toasted sandwiches and a selection of home-made sandwiches complete the savoury menu. Sinclairs are renowned for their strawberry Pavlovas, while chocolate fudge cake, lemon meringue pie, coffee walnut gateau, chocolate roulade and apple pie and custard are just as fattening. An extensive list of beverages accompanies the menu. The restaurant is licensed.

As you may expect, meals are served in good quality china, Royal Doulton, while china crystal is on display throughout the room. The floor is pleasantly carpeted, while opulent Waterford crystal chandeliers add that touch of excellence. The soft two tone pink walls are restful to the eyes. The Coffee Shop holds 64 at 19 tables and also has baby facilities. This is an up market coffee shop and although prices are a little on the high side, the service, location and food fully justify the charges.

Opening Hours: 10.00am – 3.00pm, Monday, Tuesday and Wednesday; 09.30am – 4.30pm, Thursday and Saturday; 10.00am – 4.30pm, Friday; Closed on Sunday and Bank Holiday Mondays. Phone: 01777 709670.

Chesterfield Canal

The Chesterfield Canal was a bold and imaginative concept of the early years of the Industrial Revolution. Built for the prime purpose of transporting Derbyshire coal to new markets, many other cargoes were also carried. James Brindley, the celebrated engineer, was responsible for the canal, which opened on June 4th 1777. In its time it was a magnificent piece of engineering, containing the country's longest tunnel at Norwood. Also one of the earliest examples of a large staircase of locks was at Thorpe Salvin.

100 years after the opening of the canal, railways developed and traffic began to decline. Gradually the canal deteriorated, then, in 1907, the final collapse of part of Norwood Tunnel isolated the Derbyshire section. Small cargoes struggled on for many years, finally ceasing in the 1950s.

Today, 26 miles of canal is navigable from West Stockwith, where it joins the River Trent, to Worksop. The remaining 20 miles to Chesterfield are the focus of current restoration schemes. While much of the Chesterfield Canal is temporarily abandoned, the towing path, sometimes diverted, remains throughout the 46 miles. The towing path has been named The Cuckoo Way, after the unique vessels, which reputedly were known as cuckoos that plied the Chesterfield Canal. It is possible to walk the entire length of the towpath.

Retford

The first documented evidence of the existence of 'Retforde' is to be found in the Domesday Survey of 1086, following the Norman Conquest. It is widely held that this reference was to West Retford, which existed earlier than its neighbour, East Retford. The Borough of East Retford was established in about 1105. In 1246 East Retford was granted a Royal Charter by Henry III.

In 1608 the Pilgrim Fathers, as we know them today, were forced to flee from this area to Holland to escape persecution by James l , owing to their Puritan non-conformist beliefs. In 1620 they sailed from Plymouth to America on board the Mayflower to create the first confederation of colonies in the New World.

Throughout the 18th and 19th centuries, East and West Retford prospered, with the coming of the Great North Road (1766), the Chesterfield Canal and the railways. The town's grand Georgian and Victorian buildings and large number of coaching Inns bear witness to its prosperity. In 1878 East and West Retford became a single borough.

The Market Square has many fine Georgian buildings to admire, having been laid out in the late 18th century, following the re-routing of the Great North Road through the town. The Town Hall was built in 1868 to replace a Georgian Town Hall on the north east-side of the Square. St Swithun's church, East Retford was founded in the 12th century. Unfortunately the tower of the church collapsed in 1651, demolishing much of the original building. Most of today's church was re-built in Victorian times. The building has beautiful Victorian stained glass windows.

Bassetlaw Museum, Retford.

Amcott House has been restored to its original Georgian splendour housing Bassetlaw's museum in Retford. It offers the visitor a unique chance to wander freely from room to room, to study the architecture, and gain an insight into what it would have been like to live in a fine large house of this kind , in the 19th century.

The house dates from 1770 – 1780, but from the restoration work carried out, it is known that an earlier house stood on the site from the 17th century. The first house was owned by the Wharton family until 1801. Local MP Wharton Amcotts re-built the house in about 1780 as his town residence. The house changed hands on several occasions, with the most notable owner being Stephen Peglar, a director of his family's Northern Rubber Works in the 1870s. On his death in 1937, Amcott House was purchased by the former East Retford Rural Council for use as Council offices. In 1974, following local government re-organisation, it passed to Bassetlaw District Council, finally opening as a museum in 1986.

The Route

With your back to a row of shops, walk away from the bus station as far as Arlington Way. Turn right, cross New Street to reach a flight of steps that lead down to the Chesterfield Canal.

Once on the canal towpath, turn left, go beneath the road-bridge and walk ahead alongside a bank of trees that line the edge of a pretty green park. Mallards and Coots frequent this part of the canal and will gratefully receive any crusts of bread that you can muster.

Go beneath Bridge No 57, by the Packet Inn, following a wide sweep of the canal to the right heading away from Retford. The Leverton hills form a pleasant background to the canal as it twists its way ahead. Do look out for birds, water fowl and small animals that have made the canal their home.

Pass beneath Welham Bridge, No.59, that takes the A620 across the canal.

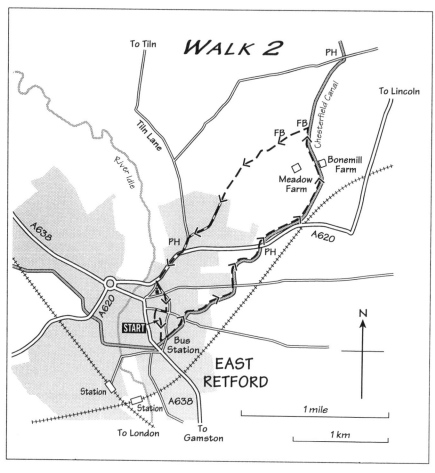

Here the Hop Pole public house on the opposite bank provides a refreshing stop should you feel so inclined. The towpath now offers many sweeping views on both sides of the water's edge of this magnificent countryside.

Ignore a public footpath signpost on the left, continue on to reach a wide grassy area at Whitsunday Pie lock. A seat has been provided for walkers to stop and drink in the beautiful surrounding. Go beneath Bridge No. 60 to re-join the grassy towpath, while to the right is the Retford to Gainsborough and Lincoln railway line.

The towpath takes you under a farm bridge that links the farmhouses of Meadow Farm and Bonemill Farm together. A wonderful lush springy grassy towpath now takes you through captivating scenery, and even on the bleakest of days, the views will give a warm feeling inside.

Walking through the gorge at Creswell Crags

The Route

Cross the large car park at the entrance to the garden centre to join the access drive. Walk back to the gatehouse at the start of the drive on the A60. Turn right passing a large sign for Welbeck College, and walk along the road for ¼ mile to come to a lone stone built house, where the Robin Hood Way crosses the busy road.

Turn right at the public footpath signpost to join a private access road, which has a right of way for walkers. Continue along this road as far as Oaksetts Lodge, where you need to cross a track and locate a blue waymarker arrow on a post at the start of the agricultural fields. An obvious concrete track leads ahead through the field to the next track. Cross, continue ahead as directed by the public bridleway signpost bearing slightly round to the right. At the next public bridleway signpost, turn left, join a grassy track to walk alongside a large plantation. Go past the college sports ground then alongside a wood. Turn right onto an access road through the wood then left at a waymarker post, marked with a Robin Hood Way symbol. Glimpsed through the trees on the left is Gouldmeadow Lake. You need to turn left onto the next track, which will take you across the lake.

Continue along the track emerging out into open farmland where a broad grassy path runs ahead. This green path is where the underground tunnel ran from South Lodge to the Abbey. There are superb views across Welbeck Park to breathe in, while the top of the Abbey, can be seen briefly in the trees. At a small wood, turn left through a wooden hand-gate and follow alongside a fence on a path which brings you to the South Lodge.

Turn left onto a track passing by the tunnel mouth at South Lodge. The track gives way to an access road, which is known as Broad Lane that connects the lodge with the A60. A pleasant walk along this quiet access road will bring you to a public footpath signpost on the right, Worksop ½ mile. Here you turn left, there is no public footpath signpost, and cut diagonally across the corner of the field to a large gap. Turn right into the next field, then, with a hedge, right, walk ahead.

Head for Sloswicks Springs wood and pass through a large hedge gap in the right-hand corner of that field. Go through a small gap in the hedge then left across the corner of the field to a small gap in the hedge. Then turn right to walk alongside close to the hedge. Go slightly left to a large gap by a tree to enter the next field. Follow the field perimeter path around to the left where footpath notices affixed to trees confirm the route. Walk alongside Walling Brook then at the end of the scrub land, turn left over a wooden footbridge to join a field path adjacent to a hedge. Bear right across the field to a hedge gap then halfway down the next field, turn left into another field crossing diagonally to the bottom hedge. A stile is set in a short piece of wooden fence. Cross one more field to a public footpath signpost next to the A60.

Turn left, walk along the busy road to a 'T' junction. Turn right, follow the road into Belph to a lane on the left that goes into the tiny village. At the end of the lane, turn right, passing Springfield Cottage to a public bridleway signpost hidden in a hedge. A grassy path leads ahead, by a fast flowing gurgling stream, which is enclosed.

Locate a stile above the stream, climb, follow the path in the same direction above the stream. Return to the low-level path next to the stream, then cross, walking along a grassy track to a road. Turn left, pass Penny Green cottages and continue along the road for 150m to reach a stile set in a wooden fence.

Follow the path up onto the top of a disused tip where an obvious path runs straight across the former coal tip. This gives an insight into how man has scarred the landscape. The lunar-looking path continues ahead over the tip and sight of this will provoke a thought or comment from the most placid person. A stile leads you out onto the B6042 where you need to turn right and walk along Hennymoor Lane as far as the road junction. Turn left onto Crag Road, then go through a hedge gap to join an obvious field perimeter path ahead. Turn right by a set of gates at Hennymoor Farm, to cross the field into a wood. Turn right onto a pleasant woodland track following as far as the Visitor Centre at Creswell Crags.

Follow the direction of the sign to the crags passing through a wood to reach Crag Road. Turn left to walk alongside the lake, pausing by the information boards, to gain further details about the gorge. The lakeside path takes you deep into the gorge passing Boat House Cave, then a little later Church Hole Cave,

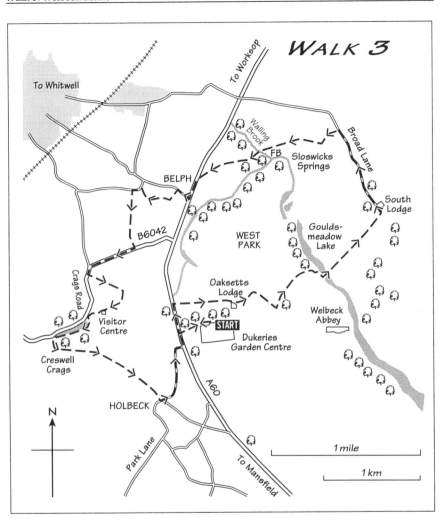

while on the opposite side is the larger Robin Hood's Cave. Go through a wooden gate to reach a public footpath signpost. Turn left, still on the Robin Hood Way, climbing to a stone wall stile.

Continue to the top of the hill where the panoramic views are most illuminating. Cross the hilltop to the next stile then descend on a grassy path to a large wooden stile. A field perimeter path takes you across the private road then along a further two fields when the path switches to the opposite side of the hedge. A short field path brings you out into the village of Holbeck. Turn left, walk along the road for just under ½ mile to the A60. Turn left, then in 150m turn back into the Dukeries Garden Centre for a well-deserved pot of tea.

Walk 4. Clumber Park

Route: Olde School Tea Room – Carburton – Clumber Park – Hardwick – Clumber Lake – Clumber Bridge – Carburton – Olde School Tea Room

Start: Olde School Tea Room, Carburton. Grid reference 606727.

Distance: 6 miles.

Maps: OS Landranger 120, Mansfield, Worksop and surrounding area; OS Explorer 28, Sherwood Forest.

Terrain: Park roads and woodland paths. Pretty lakeside path. Small amount of road walking. No climbs or inclines.

Public Transport: Carburton is served by buses from Worksop/Ollerton/Nottingham operated by Stagecoach East Midland, daily approx. every 2 hours. An occasional Worksop – Tuxford service calls at Clumber Park and Carburton, operated by Unity Coaches.

By Car: Carburton is located close to the B6034 Worksop to Ollerton road, reached from the A616 turning off just north of Budby from the Ollerton roundabout. No parking allowed at the tea room, but there is sufficient room along the road outside by the crossroads.

The Tea Shop

The Olde School Tea Room is located at the crossroads with the B6034 and the road to Clumber Park. Situated within the shadow of the park, the tea room is extremely popular with visitors to this beautiful area. Mrs Gwen Elliott has been running this tea room for over a decade and still enjoys every minute of her working day. She sees her establishment as a meeting place for many local people and visitors who love the peace and quiet of a country tea room, where the views around are most outstanding.

Housed in a former school building, built in the early 1930s, the school served the area of Carburton until closure in 1975. Gwen converted the building into a tea room with as little change to the fabric as possible. The spirit of the school lives on by retaining an old school desk in the entrance. A blackboard on a school easel contains the extensive menu, while the old school shelves have been brought into service to display woodwork crafts, hand-made clocks from nearby Whitwell, greetings cards and hand-made prints by local artists. The original children's washbasins are retained in the toilets.

Gwen tells an interesting story about the old shelves. It appears that when the conversion work of the building was well underway, one day an old pupil of

Walk 7. Teversal

Route: Teversal Trail Visitors Centre – Teversal – Teversal Trail – Batley Lane – Teversal Trail – Teversal Trail Visitors Centre

Start: Teversal Trail Visitors Centre, Camarvon Street, off Fackley Road, Teversal. Grid reference 479614.

Distance: 4¼ miles.

Maps: OS Landranger 120, Mansfield, Worksop and surrounding area; OS Pathfinder 779, Mansfield (North) and part of Sherwood Forest.

Terrain: Easy walking along old railway track beds – Teversal Trail. Enjoyable walk through Teversal village. No hills to climb.

Public Transport: Clay Cross/Tibshelf/Sutton in Ashfield/Mansfield/Nottingham service calls at the Camarvon Arms, Teversal, hourly, operated by Trent Buses. Monday – Saturdays. No Sunday service.

By Car: Teversal is best approached from Junction 28, M1. Take A38 towards Mansfield turning onto B6027 to Huthwaite. Follow road signs for Tibshelf but turn right onto B6014 for Teversal. The Visitors Centre is signposted along this road. There is ample free parking directly outside of the Visitors Centre.

The Tea Shop

Within the Visitors Centre is a small tea room, which has been operating since 1993. Staffed by friendly volunteers and run by a committee answerable to Ashfield District Council, the tea room provides welcome refreshments and hot snacks to the many walkers, cyclists and visitors. Inside the log cabin visitors centre there is room for about 30 at the tables. A further six picnic tables provide additional seating outside, giving the ideal opportunity to rest and refresh, before or after a walk. The menu is limited to snacks and drinks.

Being non-profit making, the real selling points of the tea room are the prices and the convenience of being able to get a 'cuppa' and something filling quickly. Everyone is extremely helpful with nothing too much trouble. Walkers with muddy boots are made welcome, as are dogs of all shapes and sizes. On summer weekends the tea room is very busy but it is quite acceptable to spill over into the picnic area to enjoy those hard earned refreshments. Opening Hours: 11.00am – 3.00pm, Open 7 days a week. Phone: 01623 442021.

The 'Coal Garden'

Teversal Trail Visitors Centre

The Visitors Centre is located at an ideal access point to the Pleasley Trails Network, offering a wide variety of local information on both the trails and other attractions in Nottinghamshire. Opened in 1993, on land held in Trust for British Coal, help and advice is always available from one of the volunteers or trail wardens who staff the centre, seven days a week. The centre has an informative exhibition of photographs showing how the area used to look when the coal mines at Silverhill and Teversal were in operation. There is a small bookstand of local publications and free leaflets about the trails. School parties are welcome and well catered for with specially prepared work packs. Guided walks take place at regular intervals – booking is essential. Craft fairs, shows, special events and exhibitions take place throughout the year and the centre is available for public hire to hold meetings and events.

Between the Visitors Centre and the entrance to the trails a "Coal Garden" has been developed. Artefacts such as pit wheels from the local colliery, imaginatively placed, have been colourfully painted and make a most interesting way of preserving the memory of the local mining industry.

Teversal

The "olde worlde" village of Teversal is charming, standing on a green hilltop, close to the Derbyshire border. Old Teversal is most picturesque with its fine manor, which once belonged to the Molyneux and Carnarvon families. The village is completely unspoilt and has connections with Lord Carnarvon of Tutankhamun fame. It was also the fictional home of D.H. Lawrence's "Lady Chatterley" who supposedly met the gamekeeper, Mellors, in the woods around nearby Hardwick Hall. Many believe that Lawrence lived in Teversal for a short time and wrote part of the novel during his stay there.

St Katherine's church dates from the 12th century, although the aisles with their square squat pillars are 13th century. The tower was added in the 15th century. The inside was refitted in the 17th century. Notable is the squire's pew with canopy, Christening pew, box pews, hatchments and memorials. There are eight Molyneux hatchments, the last being added in 1876.

The Pleasley Trails

The Pleasley Trails Network is made up of three different trail systems, the Meden Trail, the Rowthorne Trail and the Teversal trail. These follow the track beds of disused railway lines through West Nottinghamshire and North East Derbyshire. The original railway track was laid by two companies, the Midland Railway and the Great Northern Railway to serve the collieries at Teversal, Pleasley and Silverhill.

The Midland Railway opened the first line to the now closed Teversal Colliery in 1866. The line was later extended to Pleasley in 1877 and now forms part of the Teversal Trail. The line was continued to Mansfield Woodhouse in 1886, part of which is now the Meden Trail. The Midland Railway was also responsible for the construction of the Hardwick Junction line, that is now the Rowthorne Trail. The line running north from the Skegby car park to Pleasley and left-hand fork to the former Silverhill Colliery, was built by the Great Northern Railway, between 1897 and 1900. Today, this is the Teversal Trail.

In the late 1930s, the Midland lines were used for freight only, apart from holiday excursions until the 1960s. The first to close was the Rowthorne Trail section in 1938, the Meden Trail line closed in 1965. The Great Northern lines were open to passenger traffic until 1956, the lines closing completely in 1968. However, the small section between Teversal and Pleasley lasted until 1978, the track being lifted in 1982.

The trails run through attractive countryside taking you along high embankments and sometimes in sheltered cuttings. There are wide views of the area to stop and savour. Paths cut through magnesian limestone, with the routes being an important corridor for wildlife. The Trails are protected as Sites of Special Scientific Interest as they support good examples of Caleareous grassland, nationally a very rare habitat. As well as plant life, the Trails Network also attracts a wide range of birds, butterflies and other insects. Especially look out for Green Woodpeckers, common blue and Brimstone butterflies.

The Route

Head for the coal garden from the Visitors Centre passing through the excellent display of machinery, which is associated with the coal mining industry. Go through a wooden swing gate to join a woodland path, ignoring the Teversal Trail that runs to the right. Turn left, pass beneath the former railway bridge, to find a public footpath signpost on the right.

Climb the stile, walk ahead along a path that runs adjacent to the old railway embankment enclosed by an umbrella of trees. Cross a stream, then go straight uphill on a well-trodden grassy path still close to the embankment. A stile by a public footpath signpost leads you out onto the road. Turn right, walk along the road passing beneath the old railway bridge before going sharply uphill into Teversal.

Turn right onto Buttery lane signposted to Mansfield. Make your way into Old Teversal, which is steeped in history, passing School House Cottage. The road is tree lined on both sides and this part of the village is very satisfying to walk through. At St Katherine's church, turn left at a public footpath signpost. Here, there are two paths that start from the stile and you need to take the path that goes to the left downhill. Climb the stile into the next field, continuing ahead in the same manner, to reach the road.

Once on the road, turn right, go uphill for ¼ mile to come to a metal public footpath signpost. Go over the stile to join a thin path that is bounded by a hedge on either side. Walk ahead enjoying the enchanting views, although the large overgrown slag heap reminds you that this area has been largely associated with coal mining. At a bridge over the old railway, cross, then descend the steps to join the Teversal Trail.

Turn left onto the old track-bed and walk away from the bridge. This section of the trail has trees on either side, with their branches meeting in the middle over the trail giving the impression of a tunnel. As you walk along the trail, do keep a careful eye on both embankments, as there are many different species of birds to be spotted darting in and out of the branches.

The trail is diverted from the old railway line uphill to Newbound Lane. Turn right, cross the road bridge, then descend to re-join the trail continuing ahead in the same direction. No instruction is needed as the trail stretches out ahead rising slowly in the process. There are marvellous views to drink in for the next ¾ mile before leaving the trail at Batley Lane. On the left is the start of the Rowthorne Trail but alas is not included in this walk. This will have to be discovered another time.

Join Batley Lane, turn right and walk along the road beneath the bridge that takes the Teversal Trail towards Pleasley. Continue for a further 250m to another old railway line, also part of the Teversal Trail. Climb the steep embankment onto the trail, then walk ahead. This part of the trail is quite high and gives magnificent views of the surrounding countryside, probably at its best during Spring or Autumn. From the trail the whitewashed farmhouse at Newbound Farm is seen.

For the next mile, walk along the disused railway line, alone with your thoughts enjoying the surroundings. Ignore a public footpath signpost and steps that lead down off the trail, continuing ahead for a further ¼ mile to a

Coach Tour U.K. Silver Spoon for service. Ollerton Mill tea shop is a member of the Tea Council's Guild of Tea Shops.

Opening Hours: 10.30am – 5.00pm Tuesday to Sunday; Open every Bank Holiday March – November. Phone: 01623 822094 or 01623 822469.

Ollerton Watermill

Step back in time and visit Nottinghamshire's one remaining working Watermill. It has been in the Mettham family since 1921. The family have been millers for many generations, and have traced their history back to Kneesall Windmill, in 1635.

Ollerton Mill stands on the River Maun in the centre of the village. Built in 1713, on the site of a Domesday Mill, this red brick building, 3 storeys high, belonged to the Markham family of Ollerton Hall. The Mill has been restored to working order by the present generation of the family. It now works the same as it did nearly 300 years ago. Robert Mettham and family offer you the chance to 'Experience what life would have been like for a working miller in the early 18th century'.

An exhibition area has been erected with colourful display panels, which tell the story of Ollerton Mill from Domesday England to present day. A video shows the Mill grinding and producing flour. The large iron waterwheel seen at the entrance to the building was built in 1862. There is also a large viewing panel through which to see the wheel and race. This is still called the 'new wheel' as it replaced a much earlier wooden wheel. Ollerton Mill is open Tuesday to Saturday 9.30am – 6.00pm with the Mill working on Sundays and Bank Holidays 12.30pm – 4.30pm. Telephone 01623 822469.

Ollerton

Originally known as 'Alreton' or 'Allerton', the name means a farm among the alders. There is a tree, which can still be found growing by the banks of the River Maun. The village at one time had three watermills and was an important meeting place for influential people, as it stood at the crossroads of three coaching routes. This led to the development of the coaching inns, the Hop Pole and the White Hart. The parish church of Ollerton is dedicated to St Giles and the present building dates from about 1777. Nearby is Ollerton colliery, which closed in 1994. The site is now being developed as the Sherwood Energy Village, which is receiving world-wide interest due to its innovative environmental benefits and ethical values.

Wellow

Wellow is one of the prettiest villages in Nottinghamshire, with extensive views of Sherwood Forest. The village is most famous for its green where there is a permanent Maypole. It stands 18.9m (62 feet) high with the present steel maypole erected in 1976. Earlier ones were of timber from Sherwood Forest but were prone to being blown down in severe gales. The parish church of St

Swithin, much-restored in 1878, dates from the 14th century. The clock face on the tower was made and erected by local craftsmen to commemorate the Coronation of Queen Elizabeth II.

The Route

From Ollerton Mill, walk away from the River Maun and the picturesque small park, towards the parish church of St Giles. Ignore the road on the right by The White Hart and continue through the village as far as the A616.

Turn left along the road towards Tuxford, quickly finding a public footpath signpost at Middlefield Lane. Walk along the track that leads alongside a row of exceptionally beautiful houses and gardens, to reach a bridge over a railway line. Cross, turn left at the next public footpath signpost by the entrance to Fairholme Mobile Home Park, and join an obvious grassy path ahead.

The Maypole at Wellow

At the next public footpath signpost, the path becomes enclosed by a hedge and fence. At an obvious junction, turn left onto a field perimeter path which is adjacent to a wire fence. The path now goes in the shadow of a grassed over slag heap of an old colliery, which has, in its own way, contributed to the terrain. Continue ahead in this manner enjoying the far extending views of the pleasant undulating landscape, until reaching the end of the footpath.

Emerge onto Wellow Green, then at the road junction, turn right. Walk beneath the railway bridge before going slightly up hill to the road junction with the A616. Turn left, passing a fishing lake to walk into the village of Wellow, admiring Wellow House School on the way. Opposite the Durham Ox turn right onto Eakring Road, where the giant maypole on the green stands proud.

In 100m, turn right onto a track that leads to the playing fields. At a waymarker post, cross to the left-hand top corner of the field to pick up the footpath. Climb two stiles in close succession to enjoy a walk along a grassy field, close to a wire fence. On reaching a track, do look out, as the horse gallops here are in constant use, as a notice explains.

Surprisingly, you now have to descend 70 steps, set into the embankment of an old railway line. The track bed may be wet, but the disused railway cutting is

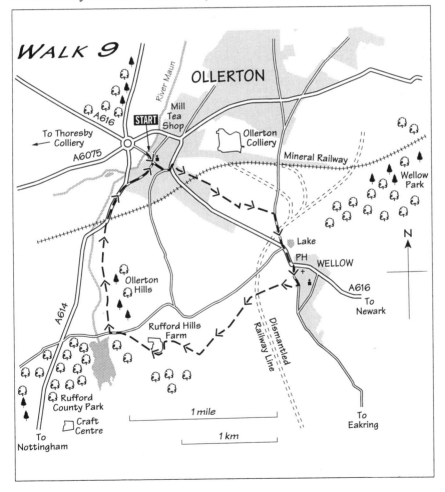

a superb venue for flora and fauna. Ascend 74 steps to the top of the embankment, on the opposite side, to continue with the walk. A path crosses the next field slightly at an angle, where there are further lovely views to saviour. Continue ahead, as waymarked, to come to a farmers track and public footpath signpost.

Turn right onto the track noting Wellow Lodge Plantation out to the right. Turn left by a pond, at a junction of farm lanes, and continue to the entrance to Rufford Hills Farm. Do not enter the farm but turn left over a stile, as directed by a signpost. Follow the path around the farmhouse and buildings, turning right at the next public footpath signpost. Walk ahead passing through a wooden farm gate, ensuring that you close the gate, ignoring a stile on the left. Pass through a pair of large farm gates by a beautiful Horse Chestnut tree, to re-join the farm access track that drops downhill to the road.

Turn left and walk along the road, noting an extremely large sign for Rufford Park Golf Centre. After a row of brick built cottages is an entrance for Rufford Mill and Country Park. Do not turn into the country park, as there is a different walk in this book (see walk no. 11) that explores the delights of the area. Turn right at a public footpath signpost for Ollerton 1¼ miles.

Walk along the field perimeter, close to a hedge, enjoying the magnificent views of the woods that grace the slopes of Ollerton Hills. In spring and autumn these woods look most colourful. The footpath, in due course, moves over to the other side of the hedge, but is never very difficult to recognise. Ahead is Thoresby colliery, near Edwinstowe, which is still very much in use, although many pits in this area have now closed. In summer this path will be overgrown but never the less quite passable.

At the A614, turn right, pass beneath the railway bridge and walk alongside the busy main road into Ollerton village. After 300m, turn right at a brown information road sign for Ollerton Watermill. Walk along Station Road, then through the interesting village as far as a road junction by the church. Turn left, where in 200m, the watermill will be found and the experience of an Ollerton Mill cream tea awaits.

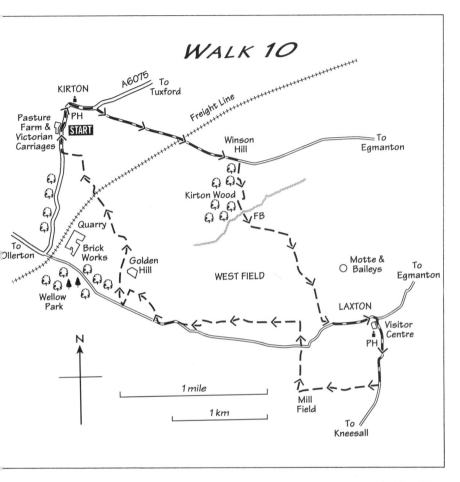

Follow the field path around to the right, then to the left, into the next field, still keeping adjacent to a hedge.

A farm grassy track now leads you onto a more defined track, where you need to turn left. Walk along this track, uphill, passing the entrance to the farm to reach a junction. Turn left and now head for Laxton along an access road. At a 'T' junction, turn left, walking into the village, perhaps calling at the dominating church.

At the village green turn right towards Kneesall, noting the Visitor Centre and Dovecote Inn. Continue along the road out of Laxton bearing right at the road junction, passing Kneesall Cottage, the last house in the village. Ignore a public footpath signpost by a farm lane, continuing on for a further 200m to the next signpost. Turn right, pass through a double wooden gate, to join a wide farm track bound by a hedge on each side. At the obvious end of the track pass through a new wooden gate to join a grassy path of tunnel like appearance. The path takes you through an umbrella of overhanging trees then, after 200m, you emerge into a field.

A grassy path has been left between two fields and from here there are fine views of the Open Field System. The path takes you up onto Mill Field to reach a farm track. An information board, left, gives details of the field you have just crossed. Turn right onto the farm track, to follow to the road. Cross to a green lane opposite, which leads below a high level field and hedge.

At a junction, turn left, then walk along a pleasant grassy track which offers plenty of shade on hot sunny days. The track funnels into a path, then you emerge out into a field, where you need to keep close to a hedge. Ignore a track on the left, continue by the hedge following round the field. At a wooden stile set in a fence, climb, and join a field edge path, continuing as before. Make for a tree close to the road where a public footpath signpost will be located.

Join the road, turn right, then after 250m a public bridleway signpost will be found. Walk slightly uphill on a field perimeter path by a hedge, keeping to the right of a small wood. At a stile and public footpath signpost, turn left, and cross the field passing the tip of the wood to a farm track. Turn left, walk back on yourself virtually to the road, where another public footpath signpost stands. Join a path that cuts diagonally over the field to the hedge. Cross a plank over a ditch, then cross the next track in the same direction climbing Golden Hill, where there are spectacular views extending as far as the eye can see.

Walk along the top of the quarry, ensuring that you keep close to a high hedge, well away from the quarry edge. Follow around the top of the workings passing to the right of a small lake. Go downhill following the line of public footpath signposts through the quarry, to cross the main access track, looking out for lorries or earth moving vehicles. A path runs inside a wire metal fence. Climb an embankment to the railway line. Cross the railway bridge, then follow around to the left, walking alongside a line of tall trees. An overgrown lane in summer leads to Primrose Lane and the A6075. Turn right, follow along the road for ½ mile to the tea room in Kirton village.

Walk 11. Rufford Country Park

Route: Rufford Abbey – Rufford Lake – Ollerton Hills – Lidgett – River Maun – South Forest Leisure Complex – Sherwood Forest Holiday Village – Rufford Country Park.

Start: Rufford Abbey, Rufford Country Park, Nr Ollerton. Grid reference 647647.

Distance: 6¾ miles.

Maps: OS Landranger 120, Mansfield, Worksop and surrounding area; OS Explorer 28, Sherwood Forest.

Terrain: Easy to follow paths and tracks with several gentle climbs. Woodland walk – pleasant path around Rufford Lake.

Public Transport: A fairly frequent service from Nottingham Victoria to Worksop passes Rufford Country Park, operated by Stagecoach. There is no Sunday service.

By Car: Rufford Country Park is situated on the A614, 17 miles north of Nottingham, 2 miles south of Ollerton. There is plenty of parking available at the Country park. A car parking charge is made between April and October inclusive, at weekends and Bank Holidays and also during school summer holidays.

The Tea Shops

On this walk there are 2 tea shops both within the Country Park.

The Coach House Coffee Shop is owned by Nottinghamshire County Council being found in the Craft Centre. Housed in the former stable block, the Coach House has been open since 1978. Originally the Coach House would have been home for a variety of carriages, all used for different purposes. The building today bears little resemblance to the days when the Estates coaches were kept here. Inside there are 20 tables which can seat up to 100 diners, while outside in the court-yard are a further 8 tables. On a sunny day, this is a most lovely setting, with the Abbey and old stable building creating a medieval atmosphere.

 Prices are most reasonable with much of the menu containing home-made food. Choose from jacket potatoes, Coach House ploughman's, omelettes with side salad, pizzas, cheese and mushroom savouries, giant Yorkshire puddings and home baked pies. There are also cakes, pastries and a Rufford Cream Tea to choose from for dessert. The staff add to the ambience by wearing mob caps and pinnies and are helpful and courteous at all times.

Opening Hours: 10.00am – 5.00pm, Daily March – November; 10.00am – 4.00pm Daily December, January, February. Phone: 01623 822944.

The Savile Restaurant is also owned by Nottinghamshire County Council, having opened on 14 February 1998. It is located in the original Victorian kitchen of the Savile country home, in the restored 'Jacobean Wing'. The stone work of the restaurant belongs to different periods, some forming part of the original medieval monastery. Lavishly converted, over a number of years, the restaurant only has seating for up to 50 in the cool, but welcoming, room.

Here is a chance to enjoy the taste of traditional English Fayre in an authentic setting. All food is home-made, ranging from soup of the day and cold platters from the larder, to Harvest Platter and Abbots Lunch, hot from the oven, and a selection of other hot traditional dishes from the menu. For dessert try Cook's hearty puddings, or choose from a selection of lovely gateaux and cheesecakes. Non-alcoholic beverages and the Rufford Cream Tea are also available. A typical three-course lunch will cost in the region of £7.50 from the carvery. On Sundays the restaurant is very busy and it is a good idea to book a table.

Opening Hours: 10.30am – 4.00pm Daily, March – December; Closed January and February. Phone: 01623 822056.

Rufford Country Park

Rufford was acquired by Nottinghamshire County Council in the early 1950s. It was designated a Country Park in 1969. There is so much for walkers and lovers of the countryside to savour throughout its 60.7 hectares (150 acres) of parkland, woodland and formal gardens.

At the heart of the park stands the picturesque remains of Rufford Abbey. In 1146, Gilbert, Earl of Lincoln, grandson of Gilbert le Gaunt brought Cistercian monks down from Rievaulx Abbey in Yorkshire and founded an Abbey at Rufford. The Abbey was a complete , self-contained monastic world with the monks working completely independent from outsiders. On the dissolution of the monasteries, during the reign of Henry VIII, the estate fell into the hands of George Talbot, Earl of Shrewsbury. He was responsible for converting the west range of the cloister buildings into a country house. In 1626 the house passed into the Savile family who lived there until 1938. Many improvements were carried out to the property when, in 1679, a north wing was built on the site of the abbey church. The house fell into disrepair during the 1940s before being purchased by the County Council in 1951.

The south wing of the Abbey still remains with a notable stable block, which today houses the craft centre and gallery. Around the courtyard, the craft centre displays a fine selection of British Crafts including pottery, jewellery, textiles, glass, woodwork and metalwork, There is a book and gift shop along with a plant and herb centre. The Coach House Coffee Shop is located here. The Orangery, a restored Georgian open air bathhouse, plays host to different exhibitions during the year. There are formal gardens and a Lime Avenue with mature trees. Rufford Abbey Cistercian Undercroft is perhaps the most impressive and best preserved in England. The splendid frater, or dining

Ancient Rufford Abbey is the centrepiece of the Park

room, and the Cellarium, both have displays on the history of the monks giving an insight into their austere life.

Rufford Lake extends to 10.12 hectares (25 acres), dating back to the time of the Cistercian monks. The beautiful lake of today was created by the Saviles in 1750, both to improve the appearance of the estate, and to provide power for the corn mill at the northern end. The lake is now a sanctuary for many water birds such as great crested grebe, tufted duck, grey heron, mallard, pochard, teal, swan and many others. Rufford Mill was built in the mid 18th Century, but is was in the 1860s when the Savile family decided to go into commercial timber construction, that the buildings around the corn mill were developed. A saw mill was built which today houses the heritage centre. It stages various exhibitions with an ever changing programme, together with a shop containing a wonderful selection of gift ideas.

An interesting curiosity to look out for in the Country Park are two ice houses. Built sometime around 1820, the two ice houses were required by the Savile family to preserve a supply of ice beyond the winter months. Yew and Holly trees were planted around the ice houses to keep them in a constant cool shade. The Country Park is open daily March to December, 10.30am to 5.00pm, January and February, 11.00am to 4.00pm. Telephone 10623 824153 for further details.

The Route

With the ruins of the Abbey and the craft centre on your right, walk ahead, passing a signpost that indicates the way to the lake. A wide surfaced path known as the Queen Elizabeth Walk takes you alongside a long row of planted trees, with the branches trained along a wire fence. Turn right and continue down a few steps to reach the next country park signpost. Turn left towards the mill, along a pretty woodland path, to the next junction of park paths. Again turn left onto the 8 minutes lakeside walk that takes you by an area of woodland known as 'The Wilderness. Just to the left along this path a diversion can be made to see the ice houses.

The lake is followed closely, with the woodland path dotted with picnic tables and seats. Continue ahead towards the mill passing the Ranger information office to arrive at the mill buildings. Go to the rear of the heritage centre, then along the very edge of the water to cross a long footbridge at the north end tip of the lake. Turn left onto a path that now takes you out of the park, through a swing gate.

Cross the road to the public footpath signpost opposite, marked Ollerton 1¼ miles. Walk along the field edge path adjacent to a hedge, nestling below the Ollerton Hills. After ¼ mile the path switches to the corresponding side of the hedge, then takes you past the top of the wood that graces the slopes of the Ollerton Hills. From this path there are majestic views of open countryside, while ahead is Thoresby Colliery near Edwinstowe.

At the busy A614, near to the railway bridge, cross to the public footpath signpost opposite. Climb the stile to commence walking firstly along an enclosed path parallel to the embankment of the railway line. In summer, the early part of the path will be overgrown, which makes progress quite slow. Cross over the sturdy wooden bridge that spans Rainsworth Water then, after crossing the next stile, access is gained to an open field path.

Continue ahead, bound by railway and road, to cross a stile and farm track in quick succession, noting a symmetrical stone railway bridge. Join a farm track that rises gently ahead. After another stile return to the farm track to complete the pull to the top of the hill. From here Edwinstowe village and church nestle below. Go past the rear of Thoresby colliery signal box, then at the end of the next field, pass through a large hedge gap. The track gives way to a thin path, which still follows the embankment of the railway line.

The first houses of Lidget are encountered where a wide grassy track takes you past the gardens of the houses. At Rufford Road, turn right, pass beneath the railway bridge and walk along High Street. On the right is the Dukeries Hotel built in 1895 by Mansfield Brewery. In 1929, the hotel suffered a fire destroying the Banqueting Suite and Pavilion. Just before entering Robin Hood's village of Edwinstowe, turn left along Mill Lane towards Clipstone. (see Walk no. 8 for a walk around Edwinstowe and Sherwood Forest Country Park).

Where the railway line crosses this road, turn right about 75m before, at a fallen public bridleway signpost. A field footpath hugs the contour of the River

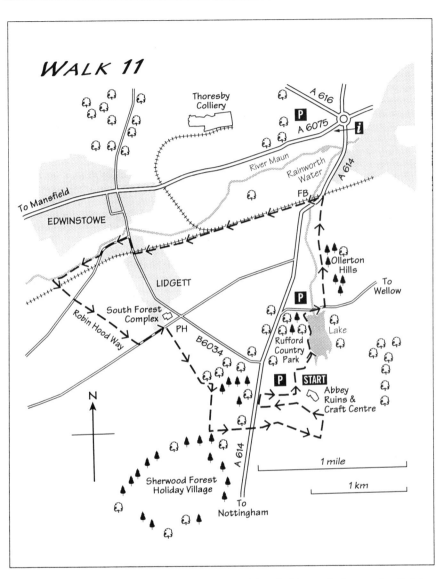

WALK 11

Thoresby Colliery

A 616

P A 6075

To Mansfield

River Maun

Rainworth Water

A 614

EDWINSTOWE

FB

Ollerton Hills

To Wellow

LIDGETT

P

Robin Hood Way

South Forest Complex

PH

B6034

Rufford Country Park

Lake

N

P START

Abbey Ruins & Craft Centre

A 614

1 mile

1 km

Sherwood Forest Holiday Village

To Nottingham

Maun, guarded by a tall hedge. At the end of this field turn left onto the Robin Hood Way, climbing slightly uphill to reach a gated railway crossing. Cross with care, then join a wide perimeter path that rises fairly amiably. At the top of the hill, do stop and look back at the panoramic view of Edwinstowe and Sherwood Forest.

Cross a minor road and rejoin the wide field edge path ahead as shown by the arm of the bridleway signpost. The route ahead runs adjacent to several fields before reaching Holly Farm. Pass the farmhouse where a short farm track leads to the B6030. Turn left and walk along the road passing Rufford View Boarding Kennels, as far as the South Forest leisure complex. If you fancy a break, continue along the road to the cross-roads, where the Robin Hood Inn will be found.

To continue the walk, turn right opposite the new leisure complex at a public bridleway signpost. The path accompanies a hedge dropping down to start with, then rising gently to the tip of a wood. A pretty woodland path brings you to a public footpath signpost on the edge of the wood. Follow the track around to the right, then head downhill still on the field perimeter to reach Sherwood Forest Holiday Village. Turn left along an access track to reach a private road within the holiday village forest. Continue along this private road for 150m to locate a public bridleway signpost. Walk along the woodland path as far as the A614.

Cross the road with extreme care to the access drive to Manor Farm. Pass by the Lodge, Manor Farm and the Old School House. The route is well waymarked with Robin Hood Way symbols. Go over a brick bridge across a stream, then turn left at a junction of tracks. In a further 200m turn left back across the stream to follow a road through an exclusive housing development to the A614. Turn right and walk along the road for 100m to the entrance to Rufford Country Park and Craft Centre. Take the access road into the park to return to the ruined Abbey.

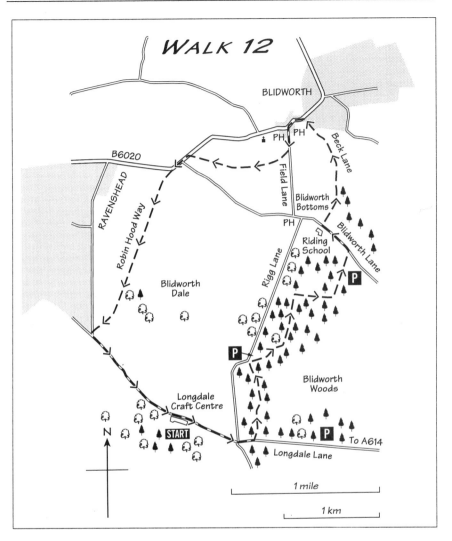

Walk past Blidworth electricity sub-station, where the track gives way to a wide field perimeter path. Go straight ahead keeping to the field edge path, adjacent to a hedge. Gradually, the path climbs again, taking you between two hedges, then up onto the top of the hill. Keep ahead, avoiding the track that goes to the pig farm, onto a grassy path by a small mature wood. A little further ahead you emerge out onto the road.

Turn left onto Longdale Lane, to pass a garage Continue along Longdale Lane passing Longdale Nursery School and Children's Centre for a further ½ mile, to return to the craft centre.

Walk 13. Southwell

Route: Merryweather Garden Centre – Norwood Park – Southwell Trail – Goldhill Farm – Halam – Cundy Hill – Southwell.

Start: H. Merryweather & Sons Ltd, The Garden Centre, Halam Road, Southwell. Grid reference 696541.

Distance: 7 Miles.

Maps: OS Landranger 120, Mansfield, Worksop and surrounding area; OS Explorer 28, Sherwood Forest.

Terrain: Well used paths and tracks over mainly flat countryside. The Southwell Trail, an exceptionally pretty disused railway line. Country lanes, with a small hill to climb at the end.

Public Transport: Services from Nottingham, Mansfield and Newark-on-Trent run fairly often to Southwell, operated by different bus companies.

By Car: Southwell is reached by using A612 Nottingham – Newark-on-Trent road or B6386 from Oxton, where this road joins A6097. The A617 Mansfield – Newark-on-Trent road via Kirklington and Halam leads to Southwell. There is a car park close to Southwell Minster. If you ask first, however, at Merryweather's Garden Centre, parking may be available subject to availability.

The Tea Shops

On this walk there is a choice of two tea shops.

Merryweather's Garden Centre Tea Room is run by Mrs Jennifer Merryweather, with help from Dorothy Manning. The tea room has been open since 1986 being housed in former offices for the garden centre. There is seating for 28 at 7 tables, where there are relaxing views onto the tree lines. Further tables can be found outside in the garden centre, if required.

The tea room has an old fashioned friendly look, in keeping with the garden centre. Lime green walls help to create this effect, with the room extremely fresh and spacious. There is an old framed photograph above the fireplace of Matthew Bramley, who sits there presiding over you while refreshments are taken. Other photographs are displayed on the walls, which are interesting to examine. A basket of toys for fidgety children is a welcome and thoughtful touch.

All cakes are home-made, with a good choice of sponges, tea cakes, Eccles cakes, fruit cake and apple tart. Do try Mrs Merryweather's carrot cake made to her own closely guarded recipe- it is gorgeous. Earl Grey tea, coffee and soft drinks are available, along with sandwiches containing various fillings, if a snack is needed.

Opening Hours: 1.00pm – 4.30pm, Monday to Friday; 10.30am – 4.30pm, Saturdays and Sundays; Open all Bank Holiday Mondays. Phone: 01636 813204.

The Minster Refectory is located in the Southwell Minster Centre on Church Street. The Centre, including the refectory, was officially opened on 24 October 1996 by his Royal Highness the Duke of Gloucester, although the purpose built centre began life on 1 August 1996. Previously the refectory was found in the kitchens of the Great Hall at the side of the Minster.

Owned by Mr & Mrs Griffin, the Minster Refectory seats 45/50 on 12 tables. The building is airy with plenty of room at your table to partake refreshments. All cakes and savouries are home-made along with many light lunches. The refectory tries to cater for most people's appetites, including vegetarians, with a warm welcome awaiting visitors. A peep at the menu shows such mouth-watering delicacies as Bramley Apple Pie, Lemon Meringue Pie, Fruit Cake, Carrot Cake and Treacle Tart. More substantial dishes include home-made lasagne or Gardener's Pie, with all prices reasonable. There is a fine choice of teas with coffee and soft drinks available. The food is excellent and plentiful. Even at the busiest of times the waiting limit for service is kept to a minimum. However due to the refectory's popularity, you may well have to wait for a table, but it is worth while.

Opening Hours: 9.30am -5.30pm, Monday to Saturday; Winter 10.00am – 4.30pm; 12.00 noon – 5.30pm, Sunday; Winter 12.00noon – 4.30pm; Closed Good Friday, Christmas Day and Boxing Day. Phone: 01636 815691.

Merryweather Garden Centre

Established in 1854 on Halam Road by Henry Merryweather, the garden centre today is currently owned by brothers John and Roger Merryweather, who are 5th generation strengths. Originally the nurseries ran a mail order business for fruit trees, then moved on to growing plants and roses. By the turn of this century it was one of the biggest rose growers in the country, with roses sent all over the world.

Henry Merryweather was responsible for developing the Bramley Apple and helping to make the apple world famous. He exhibited the apple at his nurseries in 1856, soon after recognising its qualities. History recalls that the apple was a chance seedling grown from pips planted in a garden in Easthorpe, Southwell, by two Miss Brailsfords, in the early 1800s. One pip became a tree and bore fruit and Henry Merryweather was struck by the marvellous appearance of this wonderful apple. He discovered that the cottage and garden were then in ownership of Mr Matthew Bramley, and they agreed that Henry Merryweather would build up a stock of trees at the nursery. When sold to the public they would bear the name 'Bramley's Seedling'.

At the garden centre is a Bramley Apple Exhibition, along with the history of the 'Merryweathers'. The garden centre is open 7 days a week but for details of opening hours, please telephone 01636 813204.

Southwell

Locally, the name Southwell is pronounced 'Suthell'. Situated amidst rolling Nottinghamshire countryside, this pleasant market town lies 13 miles north-east of Nottingham. Steeped in history, visitors are encouraged to take a walk around the town. Discover the beautiful Prebendal houses, (the houses of Prebendaries or Canons of the Minster) hidden alleyways and old coaching inns.

The Saracen's Head is the oldest coaching inn, being previously known as the Kings Head. This was the place where Charles I spent his last night of freedom, before surrendering to the Scottish Army, based at Kelham.

In the north of the town is Burgage Green, where Burgage Manor stands. It was here that the young Lord Byron lived, between 1804 – 1807 during his holidays, before he became famous. He was encouraged to write poetry by friends in the town and his work was published by printers in nearby Newark.

Southwell Minster is one of the loveliest but quite unknown cathedrals outside of Nottinghamshire. Founded in 956, the Minster was only given Cathedral status in 1884. It was built on the site of a Roman Villa, then re-built after the Conquest in the Norman style. It was the favourite residence of many early Archbishops of York, and the last resting place of four. The most famous feature of the Minster is its beautiful Chapter House. Here are some of the finest examples of 13th century stone carvings in England. The 'leaves' and 'berries' are world renowned. The Minster, which is also a parish church, has weekday and Sunday services. The Notice Board should be checked before entering. There is no charge, but to help maintain this great building, donations are invited of at least £2.00. Do visit the Minster Centre which, as well as the Minster Refectory, incorporates a shop, toilets and an audio-visual and exhibition area. For further details telephone 01636 812649.

Norwood Park

This magnificent Georgian hunting lodge was built in 1763. It is set in medieval oaken parkland, which was owned by the Archbishops of York, until 1778. Part of the grounds of the estate have been planted with orchards of apples and pears. Fruit growing began on a large scale in 1910. Tours of the house, park and orchards are available. Telephone 01636 815649 for more details.

The Southwell Trail

The Southwell Trail is a disused railway line, owned and managed by Nottinghamshire County Council. It provides around 7 miles of track for walking, cycling, horse riding and picnics. There are four car parks along the trail, which links Farnsfield and Bilsthorpe to Southwell. The trail passes through shady cuttings and along grassy embankments, giving fine views over the sur-

The Route

Follow the access drive from the large car park at Patchings Farm Art Centre past the farm buildings, to the B6386. Turn left and walk along the road for 150m to the cross-roads. Ahead is Calverton Colliery, opened in 1952. It still offers employment to approximately 300 workers, now under R.J. Budge Mining.

Turn right in the direction of Calverton, going slightly uphill, walking alongside Ramsdale Park Golf Course. There are magnificent wooded views north towards Sherwood Forest. Just as you enter Calverton village, which is twinned with Longue-Jumelles, turn right onto Hollinwood Lane. A wide stony track is flanked on either side by a lovely grassy verge, with St George's Hill ahead, creating a most perfect picture.

At the end of the track by Hollinwood House, filter onto a well walked thin path, which is bounded by a hedge and fence. A short climb brings you to a stile by a public footpath signpost. The path ahead now takes you onto the golf

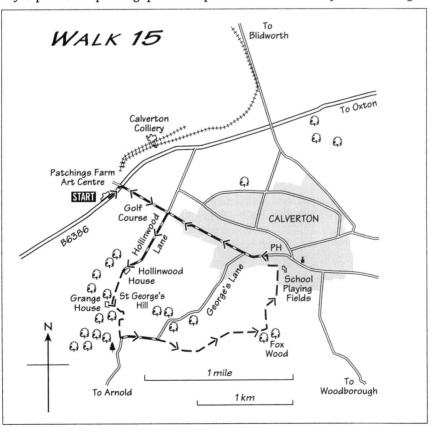

course and provided you keep close to the wooden fence, there will be no problem in crossing the course. Head for a large belt of trees above, to reach the southern perimeter of the golf course. From here do stop and admire the superb panoramic view of some splendid unspoilt Nottinghamshire countryside.

Turn left, follow alongside the perimeter hedge to locate a stile after 200m. Climb, join a stony track on top of St George's Hill and walk ahead as far as The Grange. Turn left and walk downhill on the access drive to reach the road. Turn left, follow along the fairly quiet road passing the entrance drive to St George's cottage, to reach a lane on the right on a sharp left-hand bend of the road.

Walk along the lane, which really is a track, drinking in even more magnificent views all around. The route is well waymarked and as you get further along the obvious track, the village of Calverton is seen below. In places there could be surface water on the track after heavy rain but this will not cause any inconvenience. Where the track curves to the right to Woodborough Park, turn left onto a grassy track, then right to continue ahead in the same direction now with a large hedge, right. The grassy track becomes enclosed on both sides and this may well be muddy after heavy rain. The track becomes narrower by the time Fox Wood is reached, while Calverton village is now much closer in the valley below.

Walk alongside the wood, ignoring any paths that head into the trees, then in about 150m look out for a stile on your left. Turn left, go downhill on an obvious field edge path walking in the direction of Calverton. At the bottom of the field bear right into a small wood, then the path continues between two tall hedges taking you downhill even further. Emerge out into a field and turn left over a stile. Walk along an enclosed path to reach a small pond. Keep to the tree-enclosed path, which gives welcome shade on a hot sunny day, walking alongside the school playing fields.

Pass through a wooden gate, then follow the path around to the left by the rear of a new small housing complex to reach St Clements Lodge. This is a riding school so do be prepared for horses and rider entering or leaving the stables. Turn right, walking along Wood's Lane to reach the Admiral Rodney, public house in Calverton. A large wooden statue of Admiral Rodney, situated in the car park, looks down the street keeping a watchful eye on all passers-by. However, this has not always been the case, as the head of the grotesque statue used to peer across at the cottages opposite, frightening the occupants with his staring expression, until he had his head turned.

Turn left onto Main Street and walk past the children's recreation park as far as the cross-roads. Ignore the road to Arnold, continuing through the village passing many beautiful houses. At the end of Calverton, Hollinwood Lane will be encountered once again. This time ignore, unless you fancy a second circuit, and now it is a simple case of re-tracing your footsteps back along the road by the golf course to the cross-roads. Turn left, where in 150m Patchings Farm Art Centre will be reached, and a satisfactory conclusion to the walk.

Walk 16: Greasley

Route: Greasley Church – Greasley – Moorgreen – Moorgreen Reservoir – High Park Wood – Morning Springs Wood – Brooksbreasting Farm – Greasley Church – Minton's Tea Room.

Start: St Mary's Church, Church Road, Greasley Grid reference 489473.

Distance: 5 miles.

Maps: OS Landranger 129, Nottingham and Loughborough area; OS Pathfinder 812, Nottingham (North) and Ilkeston.

Terrain: Field edge paths and woodland tracks – may be muddy after heavy rain. Small amount of walking along country roads. No steep climbs.

Public Transport: Regular services from Hucknall to Ripley and Nottingham to Alfreton call at Greasley church, operated by Trent buses. Limited service on Sundays.

By Car: Greasley is reached by taking the B600 Nuthall – Moorgreen road from the A610 and A6002 roundabou,t close to junction 26 of the M1. There is plenty of parking in the lay-by outside the church on the B600, unless there is a service in the church.

The Tea Shop

Minton's Tea Room is found in the shadow of St Mary's church, Greasley, located in the top room of the Church Hall. Roger and Judy Martin converted the former Sunday school room, with the permission of the church, into a tea room opening in October 1993. The cosy tea room is the ideal place to relax and enjoy a cream tea at one of the 9 tables inside, or in fine weather, outside in the pretty Tea Garden. There is seating for 50 but on busy afternoons, due to popularity, a wait is inevitable. However a table is well worth waiting for, especially on a Saturday, when the colourful spectacle of local weddings at the church can be viewed from the Tea Garden

The tea room has an olde world feeling with background music, fresh flowers and flowered curtains. The menu changes twice each year, summer and winter. All food is home-made with Roger and Judy rising at 6.30am each morning to bake the delicious cakes and desserts. A choice of fruit cakes, scones, date crunch, caramel shortcake and lemon meringue pie is just a small sample of what's on offer. Hot and cold lunches, salads and snacks, jacket potatoes and sandwiches also appear on this truly exceptional menu.

In 1997 Minton's were winners of the coveted "Best Afternoon Tea" award in Nottinghamshire, and every year since opening, an accolade has been bestowed upon them. In 1998 they were extremely proud to receive the Healthy

Living Award for Nottinghamshire in providing healthy food choices, smoke free areas and high standards of food hygiene. This reflects the great efforts made by Roger and Judy in providing quality teas at reasonable prices. To add to their busy schedule, Judy is also the church verger for 25 hours every week, and she seems to revel in this hectic lifestyle, enjoying every minute.

Do peruse and maybe purchase the home-made jams, hand-made cards and original paintings by local artists, which will offer a constant reminder of your visit to this beautiful area, known as D.H. Lawrence country.

Opening Hours: 10.00am – 4.30pm, Wednesday to Saturday; 12.30pm – 5.00pm, Sunday; Also open most Bank Holiday Mondays. Muddy boots are welcome!! Phone: 01773 710426.

Greasley

Greasley dates back to the Domesday Book mentioned as a farm and manor house. In the 13th century the de Cantelupes were the prominent family in the area. Nicholas de Cantelupe being perhaps the most distinguished of his family line. He was the founder of Beauvale Priory in 1343 and a friend of Edward III, who he fought alongside during the 100 years war with France. The King after the war gave him permission to fortify the manor house, which became known as Greasley Castle. The site of which lies adjacent to the church yard now called Greasley Castle Farm.

Beauvale Priory ruins are evident on private land, off New Road, about 1 mile from Moorgreen. It was the last Priory to be founded in the county and the first to suffer in Henry VIII's war on the monasteries. It belonged to the Carthusian order of monks who were strict and very hard working. The Priory's Robert Lawrence along with two others, John Haughton and Augustine Webster from other Carthusian Monasteries questioned the King's attitude and refused to regard him as head of the church. They were condemned to death and hanged in 1535. Today a yearly pilgrimage from Nottingham, led by the Bishop of Nottingham, visits the Priory, honouring Robert Lawrence and John Haughton, who were canonised in 1970.

The church is dedicated to St Mary with much of the present day structure the result of a re-building by Earl Cowper of Beauvale Park House in 1881 – 1886. However, the tower is mid 15th century. There are two fine medieval stain glass roundels depicting St Lucy and St Agatha, once part of Beauvale Priory. In the church yard there are a number of interesting graves including Joseph Gelstrap, the improver of the plough and Benjamin Drawater, Captain Cook's ship surgeon.

The area around Greasley is famous for being the background to many of D. H. Lawrence's novels. Greasely Church is given the name of 'Greymede' in Lawrence's first book 'The White Peacock' while in 'Sons and Lovers', it is known as 'Minton'. The remains of Beauvale Priory inspired 'A Fragment of Stained Glass' while Moorgreen Reservoir was 'Willey Water' in 'Women in Love' and 'Nethermere in 'Sons and Lovers'.

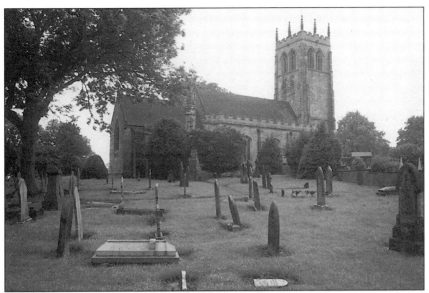

St Mary's church, Greasley

Moorgreen Reservoir

An attractive reservoir, located in a rural setting, north of the tiny village of Moorgreen. It was originally built to ensure a supply of water to the local Erewash, Nottingham and Cromford canals, although now, it only supplies the Erewash Canal. However, it is much appreciated by water fowl. The reservoir is private and can only be viewed through the trees from the walk.

The Route

On leaving the gates of Greasley church, walk along the B600 passing the car park and large sign for Minton's Tea Room, which has a good sketch of the church on both sides. At the road junction with the B6070, continue ahead following the road round past the Horse and Groom public house in Moorgreen.

As you walk through the small village there are fine views of the hilly countryside out towards Brinsley. Pass Reuben Shaw and Sons Plant Centre and Nurseries, which were started from nothing by Reuben Shaw in 1959. At the bottom of the hill, follow the road again round to the right opposite Engine Lane, walking along the road for a further ¼ mile to reach a public bridleway signpost, by the gateway at Beauvale Lodge.

Join the access drive past the lodge that leads ahead into High Park Wood. Many large ancient oaks make up the content of this marvellous wood, and in late May and June, the colourful sight of flowering rhododendron bushes line each side of the woodland track. Moorgreen reservoir can be glimpsed through the trees, sparkling in the summer sunshine.

At a public bridleway signpost, bear left away from the access drive onto an extremely pretty woodland path, that is fenced either side, and enclosed by an umbrella of overhanging trees. As you progress along this woodland path the views of the reservoir are much clearer, and it is arguably one of the best woodland walks in Nottinghamshire. Where the fence-lined path finishes, continue ahead, ignoring a path that goes off diagonally left. Continue ahead on the bridleway, passing a waymarker post and blue arrow, that continues the route at the end of the wood. The path reaches all too quickly a public footpath and bridleway junction after 250m from leaving the wood.

Turn right over a stile to join the public footpath to Misk Hills and Hucknall. A well used footpath follows around the edge of the field, then goes uphill noting a line of trees close to your right. At the next wooden public footpath signpost turn left onto a farm track, now skirting round the edge of High Park Wood. From this track the views are magnificent of rolling green uplands while the church at Underwood punctuates the skyline. Continue along the distinct track bearing round to the right, still by the wood, to pass the next wooden public footpath signpost.

At this point the sound of the M1 will be heard and seen in the distance. Ignore a grassy path off left, keeping to the ridgeway track, climbing uphill and enjoying yet more superb views. At the next public footpath signpost turn right into Morning Springs Wood. Walk ahead on the woodland path crossing over a track to join a woodland track ahead. Now the M1 is close to hand, as you make your way along the wide woodland track, descending to a public footpath signpost.

Turn left off the track joining a thin woodland path that deems to go deep into the wood. Bear left at a junction of paths as shown by the waymarker post and arrow. Continue through the wood to reach a small wooden stile and public footpath signpost. Walk out of the wood to join a field perimeter path that takes you alongside the very noisy M1. The path is extremely well used by local walkers, runners and cyclists, while the bridge over the motorway must be ignored.

Continue ahead leaving behind the M1, now walking on a path, which runs beside Callis Hagg Plantation. Do look out for Jays in this area as this colourful bird appears to frequent these woods. At the end of the path, ease yourself over a stile, out onto the road. The ruins of Beauvale Priory can be seen by walking along New Road to the right, to be viewed over a hedge. To continue the walk, turn left onto New Road and follow for ½ mile as far as Brooksbreasting Farm.

Climb a stile near to the derelict buildings and join a grassy path that runs ahead at an angle. Turn sharp left through a hedge gap and join a field path that crosses to the right-hand edge of the field. Go downhill to a bridge over Gilt brook, cross and continue along the well used field path. Walk now in a straight line enjoying the views down the Gilt brook valley and across into Derbyshire.

Cross three fields walking along the field perimeter path next to a hedge. The church at Greasley will be seen in the distance, which is your finishing goal. Follow the path round to the right, then go uphill, passing a public footpath signpost in the field corner.

Walk alongside the hedge, pausing if you wish by the wooden seat, to drink in the panoramic views laid out before your eyes. Continue on into the next field going gently downhill over two fields to reach the B600. Turn right opposite the entrance to Greasley Castle Farm and walk along the roadside back to the lay-by and church.

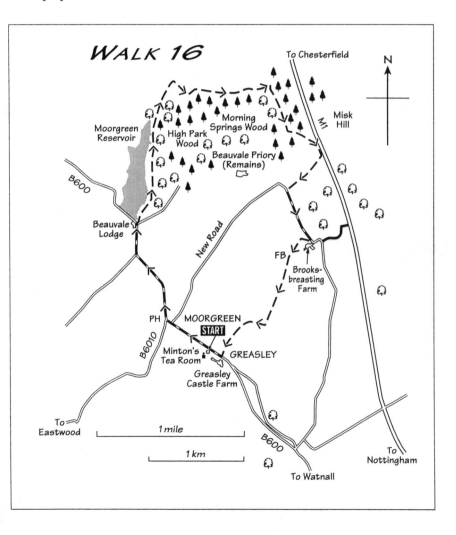

Walk 17: Woodborough

Route: Timmermans Garden Centre – Epperstone – Woodborough – Ploughman Wood – Lowdham Grange – Lowdham Church – Timmermans Garden Centre.

Start: Timmermans Garden Centre, Lowdham Lane, Woodborough. Grid reference 651478 (The garden centre is 1 mile from the village centre by the A6097).

Distance: 6 miles.

Maps: OS Landranger 129, Nottingham and Loughborough area, OS Pathfinder 813, Carlton and Elston.

Terrain: Very good paths and tracks over undulating fields. Spectacular views with several hill climbs. Well waymarked throughout.

Public Transport: Nottingham Market Square / Woodborough / Calverton (Calverton connection) run every hour during day, operated by Barton Buses. Fairly good Sunday service.

By Car: Woodborough is situated between A612 and A6097, two miles from Arnold. The village is well signposted from both of these roads. Park at the large car park of the garden centre, preferably using the overspill area to the left of the main area.

The Tea Shop

If you are looking for a relaxing 'cuppa' surrounded by an abundance of plants and flowers then this, is probably the ideal venue. Located at the rear of the greenhouse, in Timmermans Garden Centre, is Mrs Teas Coffee Shop. Christine Reid is responsible for the fine line-up of home-made cakes and delicious desserts, having taken out a franchise from the garden centre in July 1998. Previously the coffee shop belonged to the garden centre, and in all, has been opened since 1994.

Christine is expanding the menu all the time, using local produce where possible. There is an outstanding choice of cakes, scones, pies and a very popular egg custard to drool over, while in the snack range you could select from Cornish pasties, home-made pizzas, quiches, jacket potatoes and soup of the day. A Sunday roast between 11.00am and 3.00pm is available while, depending on the season different fruit pies or Pavlovas must be sampled. A good range of beverages including thick milk shakes supplement the menu. Christine is a trained chef wh bhe believes in giving value for money, as the generous portions of her servings can testify.

The Coffee Shop is a meeting place for 'locals' who enjoy refreshments, after pottering about in the garden centre. The light, airy room has seating for about

then turn left onto another field path. Continue ahead, hedge left, passing a group of farm buildings to reach the road.

Turn right and walk along the road towards the village of Woodborough. There are fine views all around, with Calverton village, seen standing on a hill, looking down on Woodborough. As you make your way into the village, ignore a public footpath signpost just before the Nags Head. Follow the road round by the pub onto Main Street, passing Woodborough Post Office, to reach a public footpath signpost on Church Walk.

Turn left along an alleyway, passing a long row of cottages, then go through private gardens, walking along an obvious thin path. Climb a stile into the pleasant cricket ground, making for a waymarker post in the trees ahead. Continue round the ground, then at a bridge, cross the stream and in due course pass through a new wooden kissing gate. Turn right as indicated along the field perimeter, then at the end of the field, turn left at a public footpath signpost. Go uphill making for Ploughman Wood, stopping to look back at the view of Woodborough village, nestling below in the valley.

Continue along a farm track to reach a junction of routes. Turn right, still on a farm track, then after 200m turn left onto a field path, that now ascends the hill to Ploughman Wood. An even better view awaits from the hill top. Walk alongside the wood, which is a nature reserve managed by Nottinghamshire Wildlife Trust, ignoring any access gates that would lead you into the wood. A well walked field path soon brings you to a hedge gap and two waymarker posts. Go ahead into the next field, then turn left at the next junction passing through a wooden gate soon after. A notice advises that you are now entering Home Office property.

An interesting path runs straight ahead over a field giving good views of the surrounding countryside and Ploughman Wood again. A small gate gives access to a farm track, which is so easy to follow. A track descends to reach an access drive from Lowdham Grange, which has to be followed for 200m. A swing gate then returns you to a field path that follows alongside a stream, probably overgrown in summer. The way ahead is very obvious, passing through a small number of gates at the start of each new field.

Cross a stream at a junction of paths, then head for a pair of large white double gates. Climb the ladder stile, cross Grange Road to a public footpath signpost opposite. Join a thin field path perimeter heading for Lowdham church ahead. The path switches to the opposite side of the hedge but is well waymarked. At the top of the churchyard, turn left climbing several steps walking away from the pretty church. A green iron railing fence will be adjacent. Go downhill, enjoying spectacular views, to reach a public footpath signpost by a large farm building. Turn right, where, in 200m the road will be joined.

Turn left. walk along Old Epperstone Road, which runs parallel to the A6097, as far as The Springfield public house. Turn left and join the busy road for 300m to the road junction to Woodborough. Re-trace your steps to Timmermans Garden Centre, a short distance away.

Walk 18: Lambley

Route: Floralands Garden Centre – Lambley – Burton Joyce – River Trent – Bulcote – Park Lane – Lambley – Floralands Garden Centre.

Start: Floralands Garden Centre, Catfoot Lane Lambley. Grid reference 617457. A shorter walk begins at Lambley Parish Church, but does not visit the coffee shop. Grid reference 631454.

Distance: 8 miles or 6 miles.

Maps: OS Landranger 129, Nottingham and Loughborough area; OS Pathfinder 813, Carlton and Elston.

Terrain: Varied walking, largely along green lanes, tracks and paths. Pleasant riverside path by River Trent. The route can be muddy in places after heavy rain. One steep climb out of Lambley.

Public Transport: Nottingham Market Square/Woodborough/Calverton regular bus service (Calverton Connection) calls at Lambley, operated by Barton Bus. There is a limited Sunday Service. Railway station at Burton Joyce, where trains between Nottingham – Newark – Lincoln call, operated by Central Trains.

By Car: Lambley is situated a short distance from both the A612 and A6097 about 8 miles north-east of Nottingham. The village can also be reached by the B684 via Mapperley Plains. Floralands is 1 mile from village centre towards Arnold and Woodborough. There is parking for 400 cars at the garden centre.

The Tea Shop

For more than two decades, Floralands Coffee Shop has served refreshments to customers of the Garden Centre. Found at the rear of the extremely large greenhouse, adjacent to the gift shop, the Coffee Shop is the ideal place to take a rest and sample some delicious home-made cakes and pastries, while at the same time, enjoying a reviving drink of tea or coffee. The Shop is run by employees of the Garden Centre, with the cakes, shortbread biscuits and scones being prepared by a member of staff. Freshly filled rolls with many different fillings are always available, while prices are very reasonable. The room has seven tables inside, seating 30 with a further eight tables outside, seating 32. A unique feature of the coffee shop is the seating arrangements. Varnished beer barrels, with a soft cushion attached, replace the ubiquitous chair. The ceiling retains original oak beams, while on the walls are many framed photographs of by-gone

Nottingham. Outside are more traditional tables and chairs; during the warmer months this patio area is very popular. Walkers are very welcome to call at the establishment and, as the floor is tiled, boots may be kept on, provided they are not excessively muddy. On a cold day, what could be better than a steaming mug of tea and a luscious home-made cake, with lashings of cream?

Opening Hours: 11.00am – 5.30pm, Daily; Open all year round. Phone: 0115 926 8137.

Floralands Garden Centre

Floralands Garden Centre is a family run business owned by W.C.Wicks Ltd. It began in 1882, as a nursery and horticultural business, and over the years has expanded enormously. Covering an area of 11.3 hectares (28 acres), 3.2 hectares (8 acres) is for use by the Garden Centre, 0.8 hectares (2 acres) for Playworld and the remainder is used for farming. For the children is Playworld, located close to the large greenhouse of the Garden Centre. An adventure playground, providing outdoor, healthy play for children of all ages. It has a great range of facilities, which help develop physical skills. It was built with safety very much in mind. There is an admission fee, telephone 0115 967 0487 for opening times and further details.

Lambley

Formerly part of Sherwood Forest, Lambley is about eight miles north-east of Nottingham. The village is set in the Cocker Valley named after the Cocker Beck, which flows through the pastoral area. Lambley is enveloped by green belt land and has almost been exhausted in growth. Its name is derived from 'Lambs' Lec' – an enclosure

Lambley from the track that leads to Burton Joyce

for grazing sheep. In the Domesday Book it was recorded as Labelia, and the place has subsequently been spelt as Lalega, Lamelaye, Lamleye, Lamlay and Lamley. Romans settled here as a medieval record refers to a byroad from the Roman Fosse Way to 'ye stretes of Lamie Woode'.

Lambley is famous for its 'dumbles'. A dumble being a local name for a shallow dale with a stream. D.H. Lawrence is reputed to have enjoyed walking the Lambley Dumbles. The tree-lined dumble is a good place for bird life and is rich in wild flowers, at certain times of the year. In Spring time the meadows around Lambley village are dotted with cowslips – a most beautiful sight.

Lambley, like many of its neighbours, was a stocking-knitting centre and in 1844 there were 400 frames in use. The importance of Lambley to the hosiery trade, at that time, was emphasised when I & R Morleys opened a factory, which still exists between 48 and 52 Main Street. Many of the cottages, used in the 19th century for this purpose, have been renovated to give the village a pleasing mix of old and new.

It is thought that the original church dates from AD1111, when a church was built to replace the one recorded in the Domesday Book. The Holy Trinity Parish church was partially re-built in 1454, by the last in line of the de Cromwell family, who was Lord Treasurer of England. If you look closely at the porch of you should see marks where bowmen used to sharpen their arrows, during enforced practice in Tudor days.

Burton Joyce

The village is bordered by a deep loop of the River Trent and backed by a ridge of rolling hills. It is a popular residential area for commuters to Nottingham. The main road (A612) divides the village from the church. According to the Domesday Survey has possessed such a building from Saxon times. Today's church, the church of St Helen, is mostly 13th century, although it was extensively restored in 1878. The nave, tower and broach spire belong to that period, while the chancel is 15th century. In the north aisle there is a tomb and effigy of the 14th century knight, Robert de Jortz. The Jortz family, once Lords of the Manor, gave their Anglicised name to the village.

Burton Joyce was also a centre for the framework knitting industry and a few cottages still remain, especially on Main Street. One famous resident of the village was Alfred Shaw, a Nottinghamshire county cricketer. He bowled the first ball of the first-ever Test Match at Melbourne, Australia in 1877.

Bulcote

Situated between Burton Joyce and Lowdham is the tiny village of Bulcote. Holy Trinity church overlooks the main A612, separating it from the village. Dating from 1862, built in the Norman style, it replaced an earlier example said to date to Saxon times. The main part of the village consists of agricultural farming at Bulcote Farm. Owned by Severn Trent, many of the fields have permissive paths around them leading to the River Trent.

The Parlour Tea Room

on display, give a warm and welcoming feeling to the room. Walkers are very welcome to the tea room but please remove any muddy boots. There is no charge to enter this part of the farm. Don't worry if it is near to closing time Johanna will look after you, as she is not in a hurry to close up.

Opening Hours: 10.00am to 5.30pm, Daily; Closed Mondays (except Bank Holidays) and end of March to end of September; Weekends and half-term week only in October. Phone: 0115 966 5037 and 0115 966 4512.

Ferry Farm Country Park

The Country Park was also opened in 1995, set in a magnificent position overlooking the wide River Trent. It has been farmed by Graham and his family for many generations, and now comprises of about 121 hectares (300 acres), which includes the country park. That part of the farm extends to 8.1 hectares (20 acres), giving visitors of all ages the chance to get to know friendly families of piglets, lambs, cows, rabbits and birds.

There is a relaxing atmosphere about the country park and children will enjoy the pets corner. Here they might like to lift and cuddle the smaller animals on the farm. Guinea pigs and poultry roam freely in this section. Ferry Farm is home to 'Arnie' the largest Italian Ox in Britain. An adventure playground provides hours of entertainment. Children love the assault course and zip line known as the death ride years ago. A pleasant walk away from the farmyard takes you around the country park, passing the wildlife pond.

Across from the Parlour Tea Room is The Coach-house. Formerly the stables for horses that worked on the River Trent, towing barges from Hoveringham to Gunthorpe. A wide range of country crafts is displayed, with animal-themed gifts and children's souvenirs. Chilled drinks, ice-creams and a selection of sweets are also available. The Country Park is open the same hours as the tea room with a charge made to the farm. Telephone for further details.

Hoveringham

Hoveringham is eight miles north-east of Nottingham, situated just off the A612 Nottingham to Southwell road. Around Hoveringham are many former gravel pits that have now been turned over to water sports clubs. A small amount of gravel excavations still take place to the north of the village. At Mill Farm, away from Hoveringham, is a three storey corn mill, with much of its mill machinery still intact.

The River Trent at Hoveringham is extremely wide due to the continual dredging of the river bed. The spoil from the river is taken by barges to Gunthorpe Lock and deposited in lorries to be taken away. At one time, a ferry operated across the river, but alas no more. In 1885 the river at Hoveringham froze over, the only time known, and villagers drove a horse and cart across.

Gunthorpe

The peaceful village of Gunthorpe was once owned by Simon de Montfort. Gunthorpe used to be connected to East Bridgford by a ferry service, and in 1875, by an iron toll bridge. The iron bridge was replaced in 1937 by a new bridge of three spans, opened by the Prince of Wales, on November 17, who later became Duke of Windsor. This is the only bridge across the River Trent between Nottingham, Trent Bridge and Newark. The old toll house near Gunthorpe Lock is now a restaurant.

Gunthorpe is steeped in history being noted for the village when Queen Boadicea defeated the Roman Tenth Legion. The village chapel of St John the Baptist dates from 1849. Today the river at Gunthorpe is a popular spot for boating and angling, with a caravan and camping site offering overnight accommodation. Side by side are two large pubs and a restaurant in the Old School House, all of which are very busy throughout summer.

Caythorpe

This tiny village is most picturesque containing a pub, post office and an old watermill. A village that grew up around the framework knitting industry, still possesses a traditional framework knitters workshop amongst the 18th century buildings. The watermill finished milling in the 1950s and has been a private house since. Studio potter Judy Firmin opened part of the old mill for visitors to inspect her beautiful pottery work. There is also a chance to view the pine wooden waterwheel in the middle of the building. Judy also make half pint mugs for The Black Lion opposite, which brews its own bitter and specialises in fish lunches.

The Route

Walk through the grassy car park at Ferry Farm Country Park to Hoveringham Road. Turn right, walk away from the farm along the road, passing a roadside car park, adjacent to the River Trent. At a public bridleway signpost go through a white metal gate to join The Trent Valley Way.

Join an extremely relaxing riverside path, where there are superb views of the wide fast flowing River Trent, and the wooded slopes of the Trent Hills, which dwarf the river. Climb a large wooden stile alongside a pair of gates and continue alongside the river. The path is beautiful in all seasons being very popular with local walkers.

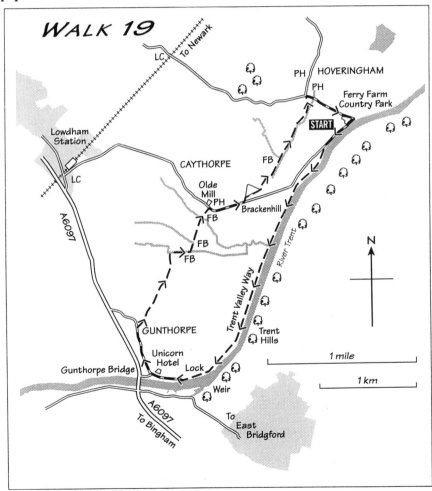

Pass through two white gates in quick succession, which allow you to cross Car Dyke, who flows into the river. Continue ahead along the riverside path close to a wire fence. In summer the river is alive with boats cruising leisurely to their next port of call. Again pass through two more metal gates within a few metres of each other, then return to the riverside path. Here a notice orders that dogs must be kept on leads so please comply. Trent Valley Way blue waymarker arrows show the way ahead to the next wooden stile. Climb and follow the riverside path to the massive and exciting weir by Gunthorpe Lock.

Bear right from the weir to reach the automatic lock gates, controlled by the lock keeper, stationed in a pine cabin secluded in the trees. The lock was purposely built in 1926 to accommodate four 27.4m (90 feet) barges that brought freight from Hull. It is 60.9m (200 feet) long and 9.1m (30 feet) wide. In 1960 the lock was mechanised, thus reducing the overall time taken in passing through Gunthorpe Lock.

Join the access road, passing the building that houses Gunthorpe Marina workshop, then the Toll House Restaurant. Re-join the riverside path walking by the moorings to reach the large Unicorn Hotel. This is a popular spot for cyclists, bikers and day trippers. Next to the hotel is Tom Brown's Restaurant and lounge bar, which is a converted school house. A little further along the road pass the Anchor Inn, then continue ahead through the village, which is most interesting as the houses and cottages are a mix of old and new.

Turn right onto Peck Lane by a public footpath sign, attached to a wall. The lane takes you into open countryside with good views of the dominating Trent Hills, away to the right. Where the lane finishes, a public footpath signpost will be found in the hedge. Ignore the track and walk ahead on a path that crosses between two fields. Pass through a hedge gap to join a wild field track adjacent to a hedgerow, to come to the next public footpath signpost and a no entry sign.

Turn right and walk along the inviting field path keeping close to a hedge. About half way along the field, turn left over a concrete one-hand footbridge across a stream. Walk ahead now with the hedge, right, crossing a wooden footbridge to continue ahead in exactly the same manner as before. Cross a third footbridge over Car Dyke, where a stile leads you out into a grassy field. From the next stile a path takes you past the Olde Mill to the main street in Caythorpe.

After a visit to the Olde Mill, turn right, walk along Hoveringham Road passing The Black Lion, to reach a footpath signpost at Brackenhill. Turn onto the access drive to locate the next public footpath signpost, just before the farmhouse and buildings. Climb an old wooden stile, set in a new fence, to tread a pleasant grassy path by the side of a hedge. At the next stile a field edge path runs for 200m to a track. Turn left and walk along the track going round to the right, passing the pink exterior of Fernhill House. At the end of the track pass through a large hedge gap into a field. Turn right and walk along the field edge path for 50m, before turning left along the bottom perimeter of the field.

Continue ahead walking by the stream, taking care in summer, as this path

post, walking ahead now making for the Nottingham – Newark railway line. Do not cross the railway line, but turn left along the field perimeter, keeping close to the line. Cross a one-hand wooden footbridge into the next field, then continue on as before passing through a hedge gap to another field. A yellow waymarker arrow affixed to the wooden boundary fence confirms the route. The path brings you to a private fishing lake, which was a former gravel extraction pit.

At a track, turn right, then pass through two kissing gates either side of the railway level crossing. Walk ahead on the obvious track that takes you past the wooden building of Thurgarton Village Hall. At the road, turn left, walk into the village passing the beautiful Maley Cottage. As you follow the road round through Thurgarton, do admire the different types of stone cottages and houses that the village has to offer. On a sunny day you could be forgiven for thinking that you were in the Cotswolds.

The A612 suddenly appears and you need to turn left, noting the 18th century Red Lion public house just along the road. Pass the Coach Houses pub and restaurant. According to the Official Deeds, the pub, garden orchard and paddock to the rear were purchased from Cambridge University on 19th June 1937 for the sum of £1050 by the Home Brewery Company Ltd of Daybrook, Nottingham. Turn left onto Beck Street where the pretty stream flows by the road. It really is quaint. Pass the Old Rectory, then where the road goes to the right, pass through a wooden kissing gate by a public footpath signpost onto a field footpath.

Cross diagonally over the field ensuring that you bear to the left of the electricity pylons. A white kissing gate allows you to join the road, where you need to turn left. Walk along the road for 200m going over the railway level crossing at Thurgarton Station. Turn right immediately at a public footpath signpost, to tread a path that follows alongside the railway line again.

On your left is the gravel extraction works, still operational, where a conveyer belt stretches for 1½ miles all around the large site, located to the north-west of Hoveringham. Ignore a stile, right, continue along the path bounded by railway and wire fence of the works, enjoying the views of the large lake recently formed by the extracting of stone from the land. Cross a footbridge spanning a stream. Continue ahead through a small wooded area, which may be overgrown in summer, to reach a small iron ladder bridge across the stone conveyer belt.

Follow along the track for 50m, as shown by the sign, then leave turning left alongside a wood. From here the full length of lake can be surveyed, which is an ideal venue for swans, grebes and coots that go about their daily business. Keep to the edge of the wood following round to the right, ensuring that the footpath is not deviated from. At the end of the wood, cross back over the conveyer belt by means of the small iron ladder bridge.

Follow along a field edge path close to a ditch, then walk over a railed footbridge across a brook. Continue ahead to come to a road. Turn left and walk

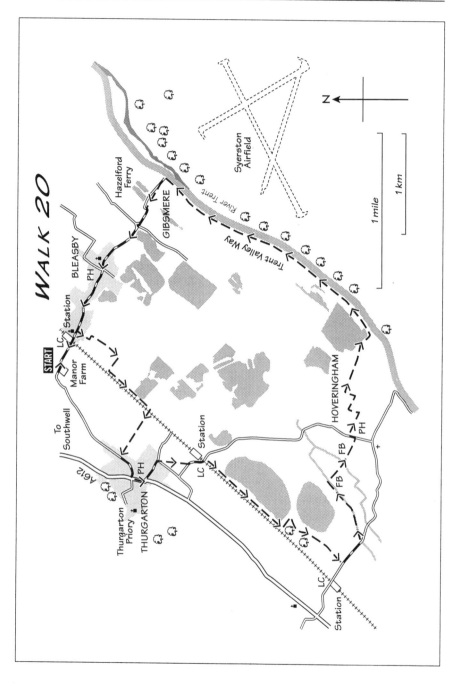

along the road for 250m to reach a bridle path on the left. Now walk alongside a stream, on a wide path, for ½ mile to locate a footbridge. Turn right, cross, then join a field perimeter path by a hedge, heading for Hoveringham village seen ahead.

In due course the path opens out into a wide track to bring you to the end of the field. Walk along the boundary edge of the cricket ground, making for a white metal gate, looking out for flying cricket balls on match days. A gravelled track leads into Hoveringham village past the Reindeer Inn, no doubt well frequented by the local cricketers.

At the road, turn left and walk along the road as far as Laburnum Cottage. Turn right at a public footpath signpost onto an enclosed path. Cross a concrete footbridge over a stream, guarded by a green gate, then continue ahead over a grassy field to the far left-hand corner. Turn left over a stile and continue along the field edge to a stile, set close to a tree. Turn right, follow a path that now skirts to the left of a pond to reach the end of the field. Turn left onto a grassy track. In due course turn right through a large gap ensuring that a hedge is right.

Continue ahead now with the hedge, left, then cut across the corner of the next field to a stile. By the sailing lake, turn right, then continue ahead to reach the River Trent.

Turn left, once over a stile, and walk along the pretty riverside path, which forms part of the Trent Valley Way. Do watch out for Herons, Cormorants and Shags that are found along this stretch of the river. The views are magnificent with the sailing lake on one side and the Trent Hills forming a perfect backdrop on the other. Pass through a double metal gate, unique to this river, and re-join the wide grassy riverside path. Another set of double gates present themselves and as you progress along the riverside path, it seems like a different world.

Cross a bridge over a stream, which flows into the river, guarded either side by a white metal gate. Return to the waterside path. Temporarily the view of the river is suspended, owing to a curtain of trees and bushes lining the route. Pass through a single white gate following a thin path adjacent to a wire fence. After the next set of white gates, the moorings of Hazelford Ferry are passed. Unfortunately the ferry has long been defunct.

Turn left onto an access road by The Hazelford, which has now been altered to a bar and restaurant together with a residential home for the elderly. An interesting combination! Walk along the access road past the caravan site to reach a road junction. Ignore the turn to Gibsmere, but continue along the road back into Bleasby. A very pleasing stroll through the village takes you past the squat church, The Wagon and Horses and Post Office to the railway level crossing. Now re-trace your steps back to Manor Farm to complete the walk.

Walk 21: Trowell

Route: Trowell Garden Centre – Disused Nottingham Canal – Robinettes Arm – Strelley – Catstone Hill – Trowell Moor – Disused Nottingham Canal – Trowell Garden Centre.

Start: Trowell Garden Centre, Stapleford Road, Trowell. Grid reference 490394.

Distance: 6½ miles.

Maps: OS Landranger 129, Nottingham and Loughborough; OS Pathfinder 833, Nottingham (South West); OS Pathfinder 812, Nottingham (North) and Ilkeston.

Terrain: Mainly level walking along well used footpaths and tracks. A pleasant long section of the disused Nottingham Canal now a trail is extremely enjoyable.

Public Transport: An excellent bus service calls at Trowell. Buses between Nottingham and Ilkeston/Eastwood and Heanor pass through Trowell or Cossall regularly operated by Trent Buses and Barton Buses.

By Car: Trowell is situated three miles from Junction 25 of the M1. From A52 Bramcote Roundabout, follow signs for Trowell along A6007 Stapleford Road to Garden Centre, found before M1 bridge. Good large car park at Garden Centre may be used for parking.

The Tea Shop

Trowell Coffee Shop, at the Garden Centre, is the Jewel in the Crown. A real gem, where mouth-watering refreshments are served all day. Owned by David Enshaw, as is the garden centre, Kath Manners, supervisor, is the main driving force behind the Coffee Shop. From humble beginnings in the early 1960s, the coffee shop has grown into a thriving business, now at the very heart of the garden centre.

Hot and cold lunches, snacks, light refreshments and drinks are available. The menu changes each day, while the variety of cakes and pastries are made on the premises by staff. A typical day's menu includes Corned Beef Hash, Hickory Chicken, Cottage Pie, Mince and Onion Pie, Quiche, Salad, Roast Chicken and Jacket Potatoes with assorted fillings. Cheese or Cherry scones, tea loaf, carrot cake and caramel shortcake are all very much in demand. Hot puddings such as: Apple Crumble or Strawberry Crumble served with cream, ice cream or custard are very popular. Breakfast special is on offer during the morning for anyone who may fancy a 'fry up' before walking. Hot meals are served between 11.30am and 2.30pm.

The coffee shop seats between 60 and 80 patrons, in a well laid out large

Sundays between 1st April and 31st October; Open all day Bank Holidays. Phone: 0115 940 5736.

Ruddington

Ruddington is a friendly village with good pubs, shops and many different eating houses. History recalls that in 1487 the army of Henry VII camped there on the eve of the Battle of East Stoke. This was the last battle of the War of the Roses. The church of St Peter was built around 1887 standing on the site of an earlier medieval building. It is well worth a visit to view this architectural masterpiece.

The village was once a busy centre for the framework knitting industry. This heritage has been kept alive at the Ruddington Framework Knitters' Museum, located in unique restored 19th century workshops, cottages and garden. It features period reconstruction 1850 and 1900 cottages and frame shops, containing the collection of hand frames which can been working daily. There is also a working collection of circular sock machines on which you can try your knitting skills. Open Easter to December, Wednesday to Saturday and Bank Holiday Mondays 11.00am – 4.30pm and Sundays 1.30pm – 4.30pm Admission charge. Telephone 0115 984 6914.

There is also a village museum which occupies part of a mid 19th century school. It depicts the community life of Ruddington and consists of several reconstructed shops: an Edwardian fish and chip shop, a pharmacist, a cobblers, an ironmongers and a toy shop. The museum also has an Edwardian schoolroom, a collection of farm implements and temporary displays. Open April 1st to October 31st, Tuesday, Thursday, Sunday and Bank Holidays in April and May 2.30pm – 4.30pm June to September, Tuesday – Saturday 2.00pm – 4.30pm with Sunday and Bank Holiday Monday 2.30pm – 4.30pm. Admission charge. Telephone 0115 940 5057.

Rushcliffe Country Park

Situated ½ mile from Ruddington, just off the A60, is Rushcliffe Country Park. Comprising 84.9 hectares (210 acres) of grassland, conservation and landscaped areas where over 150,000 trees have been planted. This park is relatively new but is taking shape quickly. There is a 2 hectares (5 acres) man made lake with adjacent picnic areas and a network of 5 miles of footpaths. It is hard to believe that, before the park, this was an army ordnance depot belonging to the Ministry of Defence.

Nottingham Heritage Centre

Within Rushcliffe Country Park is the Heritage Centre, which covers an area of 4.4 hectares (11 acres). The centre is the springboard for a new preserved railway line, which will connect Nottingham to Loughborough and the Great Central Railway line. Volunteers are busy working on the restoration of the line towards Rushcliffe Halt. The Heritage Centre is open on Sundays and Bank Holiday Mondays between Easter and October, when steam trains operate a 2 mile round trip from Ruddington Station, which takes 17 minutes. Other attractions include: a classic public road transport collection, a miniature railway, shop and other items of interest for all ages. Admission charge. Telephone 0115 940 5705.

Gotham

Gotham (pronounced Goatham) derived its name from the Saxons who maintained large flocks of goats. The suffix of "ham" being old English for meadow or home – for goats. The village was made famous because of the rhyme about wise men. The tale tells how these wise men dragged a cart to the top of a barn to shade it from the sun, burnt down the forge to rid it of a wasps' nest, tried to drown an eel in a pond, attempted to rescue the moon from a pond and most foolish of all, put a hedge around a cuckoo to shop it flying away. There was method in this madness. King John wanted to build a hunting lodge in the village until he was put off by the three men and their foolishness.

Taking a well-earned break by the old village school in Bunny

Bunny

This village owes much of its beauty to the Parkyns family. Sir Thomas Parkyn lived at Bunny Hall, built in the 17th century for the eccentric. It was also known as Crazy Hall. He was renowned for such diverse interests as wrestling, coffin collecting (he would give the coffins away to anyone who asked) and the reforms for farm workers' wages. He also built the village school, which can be seen by the gates of the 14th century St Mary the Virgin parish church. It bears the date of 1700 on a plaque above the door. Do stop and read the full inscription – it is most interesting.

The Route

Starting at the coffee shop, walk along High Street, noting the Police Station on your left. Follow the road round to the right passing the green, turning left onto Asher Lane, where the Hobbit Cottage will be seen. At the end of the lane is a public footpath signpost to Gotham, 2¼ miles.

Ignore the entrance into Rushcliffe Country Park, continuing along the lane as far as the level crossing, where the Heritage Centre railway line is crossed. Continue ahead to reach a public footpath signpost by Ruddington Fields Farm.. Climb a stile and walk along the private road to a junction of tracks. Turn right, cross the bridge over the Great Central Railway line, to locate a public footpath signpost.

Follow along the top of the embankment above the railway line enjoying the marvellous views. The path continues for ½ mile in a similar fashion to bring you to a railway bridge. Here the path goes round the field to the right by a stream to a public footpath signpost. Cross the bridge over the stream to re-join a track that leads by the railway line again. In a further 200m, a junction of footpaths will be encountered at Fairham Brook.

Cross the brook, before turning right at a yellow waymarker, then follow the meandering watercourse along a field edge path. Pass a bank of poplar trees standing proud by the waters edge to reach a waymarker post and arrow. Turn left, where an obvious path cuts between two fields and very soon a hedge accompanies you to the left. The path open out into a wide grassy track, while ahead is the village of Gotham and Gotham Hill as its backdrop.

At a public footpath signpost, turn left, then immediately right away from the track, following alongside a stream and hedge. The path is well walked and continues around the field edge towards the church, eventually bringing you to a new wooden stile. Climb, then walk along an enclosed path into the village of Gotham.

After a visit into the village perhaps, return to this point where you turn left and walk along the road to a public bridleway signpost for Leake Road. A rutted track leads ahead to a junction of tracks. Bear to the left, keeping on the same track, heading in the direction of Forge Farm. Turn right across the dismantled railway line to a public bridleway signpost to Gotham Lane.

Walk along the field perimeter path, adjacent to the overgrown railway track bed, then turn right along an irrigation ditch to a footbridge. Cross, continue ahead then pass beneath the railway bridge of the Great Central Railway line. Join an obvious track ahead, where to the right is Hotchley Hill and the British Gypsum works. Ignore a track off right, continuing along the field path

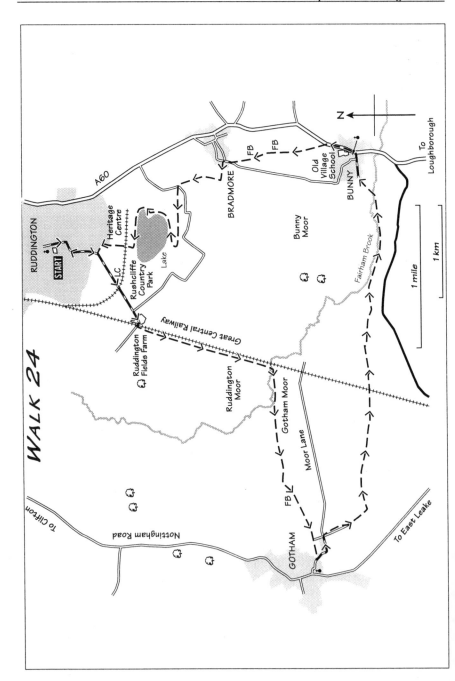

as shown by the blue waymarker arrow. This part of the walk may well be muddy after heavy rain, as it is well used by horses.

At the next public bridleway signpost, cross the field as shown, noticing the church of Bunny in the distance. Cross a ditch and walk straight ahead passing to the right of a lone tree in the field. At Fairham Brook once again, turn right and walk on the field edge path next to the clear stream. As you walk alongside the water, do keep a sharp eye open for a Heron searching out a tasty meal or a Kingfisher darting from bank to bank in a similar quest. Take a short diversion round a ditch but continuing ahead afterwards, still by the brook.

Turn left over the stream, at an interesting farmers bridge, then walk diagonally across the field to reach a myriad of public footpath signposts at the entrance to Bunny village. Walk along Main Street as far as the A60, Loughborough Road, turning left opposite the Rancliffe Arms. Pass the church gates and the old village school, then in 200m locate a small wooden stile and short public footpath signpost in the hedge.

Cross diagonally over a lush green field to a large wooden stile, where an enclosed path leads you through a swing gate, and onto the next stile. Another pleasant grassy path brings you to a wooden footbridge, which is guarded at one end by a stile. Walk along the field edge path to a second wooden footbridge and stile. Go diagonally across the next two short fields, then turn right along a field perimeter, to a stile. Pass through a delightful meadow, climbing to the top of the hill, making for the waymarker post in the left-hand corner. Turn right onto a lane and walk into the small village of Bradmore.

Turn left onto Littlemoor Lane, where a public footpath signpost and swing gate will be found. Follow the field edge path downhill then continue along the field bottom, alongside a hedge to reach a quiet lane. Cross the lane to an entrance into Rushcliffe Country Park, passing through the opening onto a gravelled path and turn left.

The park perimeter path is pleasant to walk along. Take the first path on the right to go into the heart of the park. Turn right at the next junction of paths to reach the lake. Follow round the lake to the right, passing the rangers log cabin office, making now for the large footbridge over the railway line at the Heritage Centre. The park boasts the best children's adventure playground in the county and when you pass by it is not hard to see why. Once over the footbridge, make diagonally left to leave the park at Asher Lane. Turn right to retrace your footsteps back into Ruddington village and a well-earned cream tea.

Walk 25 East Leake

Route: Manor Farm Animal Centre – East Leake – Site of St Peter's church – Rempstone – Sutcliffe Hill – King's Brook – Stanford Hall – Home Farm – East Leake.

Start: Manor Farm Animal Centre and Donkey Sanctuary, Castle Hill, East Leake. Grid reference 558256.

Distance: 5¼ miles.

Maps: OS Landranger 129, Nottingham and Loughborough area; OS Pathfinder 853, Loughborough (North) and Castle Donington.

Terrain: Well used paths and tracks over undulating countryside. The route is waymarked throughout. One hill to climb – not too steep. Small amount of road walking.

Public Transport: Good bus service from Nottingham (Broadmarsh) to Loughborough passes through East Leake. Operated by South Notts Bus – Manor Farm is 5-10 minutes walk from centre of village.

By Car: From Nottingham, take the A60 until reaching the traffic lights at Rempstone. Turn right onto A6006 towards Zouch/Sutton Bonington for 2 miles then turn right into East Leake. Manor Farm is located along this road on the outskirts of the village. Parking is available at the farm, by kind permission of the owners.

The Tea Shop

The Olde Barn Café is located within the animal centre and donkey sanctuary, at Manor Farm. By permission of the owners, Mrs Robinson and Miss Thurman, walkers are most welcome at the tea shop, without having to pay the admission charge to the farm. Opened in 1997, the tea shop is run by staff of the Animal Centre, with cooking at the weekends left in the capable hands of Mrs Pam Copeland. During the week, the cook for the day nursery prepares the food for the tea shop as well as the nursery meals.

There are 8 tables seating 32 in a well-organised run establishment. The Olde Barn Café is housed in a beautiful converted building, which was previously stables. Exhibited around the room are fine examples of old farming implements, with a wonderful Shire Horse Brass on the back wall. A feature fireplace is the focal point of the tea shop and your eyes are drawn to this delightful area time and again. The menu consists of snacks, a good selection of home-made cakes, rolls, hot sandwiches including bacon, double egg and egg and bacon and cold sandwiches. In the winter, hot soup and jacket potatoes are

The Olde Barn café

also available. A children's menu consists of a smaller version of the adults menu. Tea, coffee, drinking chocolate and soft drinks are also on sale at reasonable prices. Cream teas are usually available and there will be no complaints of the lashings of jam and cream that go with the scones!

Opening Hours: 10.00am – 5.00pm Saturday and Sunday, all year; Open Bank Holidays and also throughout the school holidays. Phone: 01509 852525.

Manor Farm Animal Centre and Donkey Sanctuary

Situated in over 40.4 hectares (100 acres), in an elevated position, on the Nottinghamshire/Leicestershire border, Manor Farm Animal Centre overlooks the surrounding countryside. The owners of the farm decided to set up an animal sanctuary in 1995 to look after a variety of animals that were not wanted. The first animal to arrive was Larry, a sheep. The owners realised that as the animal collection expanded, they needed more help in looking after them, so staff were employed. Veterinary bills and wages for staff had to be found, so it was decided that the animal centre would open to the public, but it was only in 1998 that the sanctuary started to promote itself.

There are nature trails to follow where different species of flowers can be seen in the wild flower meadow. A natural lake has been formed, where children can go pond dipping, and also discover the living willow sculpture. Children and adults can make friends with the animals, which include rare Kune Kune pigs, donkeys, horses, ponies, pet rabbits, chipmunks, peacocks and poultry to feed. All the animals are allowed to live out their full life span at this friendly farm, where the staff take time to show visitors around and nothing is too much trouble for them. Open all year round at weekends, Bank Holidays and during school holidays, 10.00am – 5.00pm. For details of admission charges telephone 01509 852525.

East Leake

Over recent years East Leake has expanded into a commuter village for Nottingham and to a smaller degree Loughborough, Leicestershire. However, it has managed to retain its village look and feel, no doubt helped by the stream that flows through the centre by the green and war memorial.

The church of St Mary the Virgin is most impressive with a 13th century tower, topped by a 15th century spire. The north wall of the naive is Norman as evidenced by two fine patches of herringbone masonry and small high windows. The chancel contains a splendid 600 year old window, while an east window in the aisle is 14th century, with glass depicting the memory of a former rector, John Bateman. Its rarest treasure for all to see is a vamping horn, which is one of six left in the country. Measuring 2.4m (7 feet 9 inches) long, this tin trumpet was used until 1855 by one of the choir to "vamp up" or drone out the bass of the hymn singing.

Rempstone

Only just in Nottinghamshire, Rempstone lies just over the border with Leicestershire, some four miles from Loughborough, along the A60. The village is strongly associated with the Rempstone family, taking its name from them. Sir Thomas Rempstone was a great friend of Henry IV and helped put him on the throne of England.

The church of All Saints dates from 1773, although it is believed that the present church in Rempstone was moved from that site of St Peter's church, about ½ mile away. This site is passed on the walk, where a number of old gravestones mark the place that once belonged to St Peter in the Rushes church. The church was pulled down in 1771 and stones from this church were used to build the present church. At this site, evidence was also found of what is thought to be a moated manor house, built over 900 years ago.

Stanford Hall

Stanford Hall was built in 1774 for Charles Vere Dashwood, a Sheriff of Nottingham. The architect was William Anderson of Loughborough. Only the central position of that building now remains, and can be recognised by the older brickwork and the "dog tooth" decoration, below the roof eaves. The Hall and estate straddles the two counties of Nottinghamshire and Leicestershire. This grade 11 listed building, set in 121.4 hectares (300 acres) of parkland, is very definitely in Nottinghamshire. In 1945 the hall was purchased by the Co-operative Union and became the Co-operative college. Many students in the first year of 1945/1946 being returning ex-servicemen. Today, the hall is internationally famous for its co-operative values that the college strives to achieve, and is extremely proud of its facilities as a conference and learning centre.

The Route

From the car park for Manor Farm Animal Centre, walk back along the farm access drive to the road and turn right. In 100m turn right at a public footpath signpost to join Mill Lane. Just before the lane ends, opposite house No. 3, turn right and climb a wooden stile to gain access to a path that runs alongside the animal centre.

The footpath has been diverted around the farm, but there is no difficulty at all in following the line of the path, as it is mainly enclosed between a hedge and fence, belonging to the animal compounds. Climb the next wooden stile where there are majestic views of the countryside around East Leake, then pass through two gates either side of the animal farm track, continuing on to the next stile. The path now crosses a very small section of the southern end of the farm. You must keep to the route ahead as shown by the signs.

A very pleasant grassy path between two wire fences lead you to the next stile, where the field edge path continues alongside a fence. Climb a stile then cross a one hand wooden footbridge over Sheepwash Brook. Turn left, following alongside the brook to reach a smaller second footbridge. Cross, rejoin the field footpath still by the brook, which is now well secluded by large trees. Go past a lake on your left belonging to Butterley Aggregates, which is private, where a waymarker arrow will be located on the stump of a gate.

Keep the lake left, as you walk ahead to come to the site of St Peter in the Rushes church, marked by many gravestones now falling backwards, drunk with time and surrounded with unkempt grass. Do spend a few minutes looking round and reading the inscriptions on the gravestones – it is most interesting. Find the stile in the hedge corner, which allows you now to join a path that crosses a large arable field. Make for the tower of the church of All Saints at Rempstone, should the line of the field path not be clear. In the distance is the East Midlands Helicopter Centre at Oaklands Farm situated near to the A60 between Rempstone and Costock.

At the A6006, turn left at the road and pass the entrance gates to the church, continuing to Rempstone crossroads. Cross the busy A60 at the road traffic lights and head along Main Street in Rempstone village. Pass a beautiful black and white cottage appropriately named 'The Thatch', then the White Lion, to reach a public footpath signpost on the right. Climb the easy stile to walk along a grassy path ascending a small hill. Turn right along the field edge, from where there is a good view of the much extended Manor House.

The path undulates as Sutcliffe Plantation is skirted past and from the next stile a really superb view of the castellated Rempstone Hall is enjoyed. Before following the path down Sutcliffe Hill, breathe in the panoramic views of Loughborough, where the tower of the Carillon can be picked out. This brick

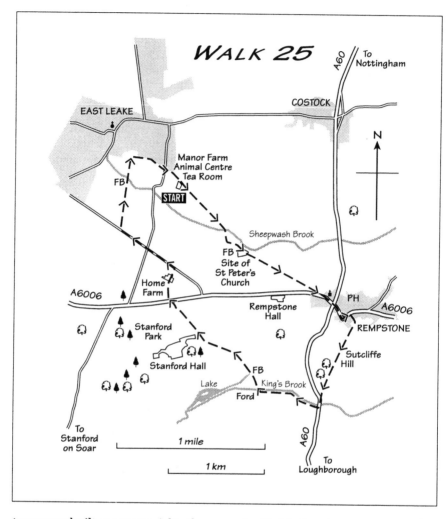

tower was built as a memorial to the men who died in the 1914–1918 war. The hills of Charnwood behind the town form a perfect back cloth. At the bottom of the hill the path cuts across the corner of the field to reach the A60. Turn left and walk along the road for 150m crossing just inside the Leicestershire border, to a public footpath signpost.

Follow alongside King's brook, where local tradition claims the brook was named because Richard III paused there to water his troops whilst on the way to the Battle of Bosworth. After nearly ½ mile, a junction of footpaths will be encountered. Turn right over the stream by the aid of the large stepping stone and pass through a wooden gate. Cross the grassy field to a farm gate opposite, where you then need to continue uphill on a farm track, which is well used by horses. On the left is the start of the lake in the grounds of Stanford Hall. At the top of Cherry Hill go through a twin gate, continuing alongside the brick boundary wall of Stanford Park. Pass through two wooden swing gates in quick succession to join a track. The top of the hall is glimpsed along with the beautiful parkland of this estate. At the end of the woodland lane turn left, and walk along the A6006, passing the entrance gates to Stanford Hall.

Opposite North Lodge turn right at a public footpath signpost to join a track that leads to Home Farm. Pass between the farm buildings and continue along the track to reach a quiet road. Turn left and follow along the road to the junction. Cross to the road opposite to East Leake, where after 250m, turn right at a public footpath signpost. Climb the stile by a small farm gate and walk straight ahead, making for the spire of St Mary the Virgin in East Leake.

Climb a sturdy wooden stile set in a fence, where a meadow path takes you to a stream. Cross the concrete footbridge over the clear stream, then after a stile, join a field footpath uphill. Keep a hedge left, ignoring a metal kissing gate in the top left-hand corner of the field. Turn right, still in the same field, and follow alongside the hedge noting the yellow waymarker arrows placed on wooden pasts strategically showing the way. Climb the stile by a farm gate to reach the road, turn right and return along the road to the Animal Centre at Manor Farm.

Tea Shop Walks — Spreading everywhere!

The Sigma Leisure Tea Shop Walks series already includes:

Cheshire

The Chilterns

The Cotswolds

The Lake District, Volume 1

The Lake District, Volume 2

Lancashire

Leicestershire & Rutland

North Devon

Northumbria

The Peak District

Shropshire

Snowdonia

South Devon

Staffordshire

Surrey & Sussex

Warwickshire

The Yorkshire Dales

Each book costs £6.95 and contains an average of 25 excellent walks: far better value than any other competitor!

Also about Nottinghamshire . . .